Brain Friendly
Language Learning

Neurolanguage Coaching

2nd Edition

Disclaimer

Any statements made in this book as to the neuroscientific research which supports Neurolanguage Coaching are made in good faith on the basis of the findings of published, peer-reviewed, scientific journals and books relating to neuroscience and brain-related texts and articles at the time of publication and not any first-hand scientific research undertaken by the author herself. In the absence of any fraud or negligence, no responsibility for any errors or omissions, or loss or damage suffered by any person acting, or refraining from acting, as a result of the material in this publication, can be accepted by the publisher or the author.

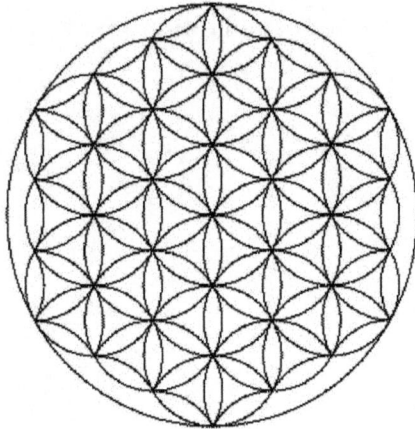

Brain Friendly
Language Learning

Neurolanguage Coaching

2nd Edition

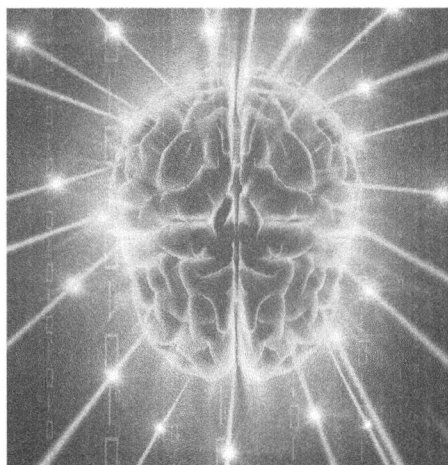

RACHEL PALING

THE CHOIR PRESS

First published in the United Kingdom in 2017 by The Choir Press
2nd Edition published 2025

ISBN 978-1-78963-536-2

"Live as if you were to die tomorrow.
Learn as if you were to live forever."

Mahatma Gandhi

Dedicated to my father, Terence Alfred Paling, 1928–2023

Contents

Part V

Acknowledgements

As I write this section in 2024, I would like to thank the original Neurolanguage coaches who did my courses and became certified and accredited over the first three years, 2013 to 2016, as they were very much the brave ones, the pioneers and the visionaries. Without them this concept would never have moved forward. I would especially like to mention Claire Oldmeadow (RIP), who, together with Mary Kennedy and the Language Network, organised the first ever Efficient Language Coaching certification course in Paris in 2013. That was indeed the very beginning!

Now, at the end of 2024, I would like to thank the whole network of just over 1,700 Neurolanguage coaches across the world. What an amazing network of heartfelt, like-minded brilliant educators you all are!

I would like to thank Claudio Tambara, who supported me from the beginning, and who created the websites and artistic part fleur-de-lis logo of Efficient Language Coaching.

I would also like to recognise and acknowledge that, without Gary Houlton and Elsa da Sousa, none of the ELC or Neurolanguage world would exist! I am eternally grateful to you both for all your dedication, passion and, above all, support to bring the vision of 'more effective and efficient twenty-first century teaching' to the world.

Neurolanguage Coaching® is a registered trademark in Europe and the US. Efficient Language Coaching and ELC Language Coaching Certification are both European trademarks registered under Efficient Language Coaching. The 3Ms, the 5Cs, the PACT PQC model and the PROGRESS model are copyright of Rachel Marie Paling. All references in this book to Neurolanguage Coaching shall be made hereinafter without the ® symbol, under the tacit understanding that it refers to the trademark.

Introduction to the second edition

The first edition of this book on the subject of Neurolanguage Coaching was well received by so many of you, and the feedback encouraged me to push on. However, there were some who took an instant dislike to this new concept and rejected it. I can understand their opinions. Language coaching, as opposed to directive teaching, was uncharted territory to be explored and developed as time went on. It took brave and open minds to believe not only that it was possible as a concrete concept, but that it could enhance and improve language learning in general.

However, I was not to be deterred. To develop this concept and ensure that it became a reality, I had to get the discussion going; like minds had to come together to effect the change.

In 2013, I created the ELC Language Coaching certification. I was one of the first to achieve the ICF accreditation for such a course and, I do believe, one of the first to crystallise language coaching into a 'system' or 'approach' or 'method', however you would prefer to call it. Shortly afterwards, the enquiries started to arrive in my mailbox, and teachers became curious and signed up for the course. Their positive feedback drove the concept forwards.

In 2017 it became obvious that an introductory book had to be written. Now that their curiosity had been aroused, teachers needed information, they needed a general introduction to the new world of language coaching, and they needed to know what training and support was offered to implement it. In short, they needed a practical guide to a new concept.

However, some academics did not seem to appreciate my 'heart and soul' style. I am not sure whether the detractors offered their criticism constructively, but I have accepted it in that manner and used it to develop my initial concept and my own skills. No one should stand still in the world of learning, and I certainly do not. More than ever before, though, I am totally convinced that Neurolanguage Coaching works, and not only for adults but for children too.

In the first edition, I touched superficially on certain aspects, and now I believe that education has recently taken a huge evolutionary leap. The COVID pandemic of 2020 caused a massive shift in education. With home schooling and sometimes a lack of schooling altogether, there was a definite need for compassion and for teaching from the heart. In addition, the last years have seen AI become more and more pervasive, impacting teachers and learners. Both of these events have caused teachers and educators to rethink many of the old educational norms, looking for new ways to keep up with progress while at the same time focusing on learner-centric education. So now there is most definitely a need for a second edition as teachers seek more knowledge on the subject of coaching in education, and in particular on Neurolanguage Coaching.

While this book now goes deeper into the subject and answers even more questions, it is still a guide, an introduction and an invitation to come to the courses, to reflect deeply and discuss broadly, to embrace the world of coaching and hopefully become convinced of its present and future potential.

This concept emerged through my own experience of teaching and through my passion for learning languages on and off over a span of 35 years. I speak French, Spanish, Italian, German and some Catalan, with basics of Arabic and Russian. I will never stop learning and plan to master Chinese and Greek as soon as I can.

In addition, my own personal development as a life coach began in the year 2003. It became quickly apparent to me that personal development was a deep dive into our emotions, senses, decision-making reactions and mental functions. In short, personal development involved our brain, and how could I study personal development without being consumed by neuroscience? Being a passionate linguist and a life coach with a burning fascination for the brain could lead to only one thing: a combination of both elements to strengthen both and produce something extraordinary. The concept of Neurolanguage Coaching had been born.

In the beginning, the most fascinating driver for me was seeing better learning results from my own clients. Now, after nearly 13 years of delivering my training, we have countless testimonials from many of the language teachers who have become certified Neurolanguage coaches. They, in turn, are witnessing better results from their clients.

I am well aware that my explanations of the neuroscientific principles may be a simplified layman's (or rather laywoman's) interpretation and not a perfectly scientific description, and some may even be based on my own speculative observations. My intention in writing this book and teaching my courses is to remove any fear and to demonstrate that neuroscience can be understood by everyone, and especially by language teachers across the world who cannot always relate to highly theoretical or scientific descriptions. My intention is also to show that understanding neuroscience and implementing it through professional coaching conversations can reap very valuable rewards.

There are many teachers who experience an aversion to science because they feel intimidated by it. Neuroscience requires only a curious brain and a desire to understand that every brain is different; that understanding the brain more can lead to a better understanding of how our students gain, process and retain knowledge.

Information can be interpreted in many different ways. I constantly bear in mind that each and every one of us is different, with our own unique perspective on the world and how we receive, perceive and interpret information.

As we understand more about ourselves, we see our potential to change our own brains and even influence our external world.

For example, many have heard the expression 'energy flows where attention goes', but how does this relate to learning? Well, one of the questions we should constantly be asking our learner is 'Where is your attention now? What are you focusing on right now? Are you focusing on the positive "yes, I can learn" or on the negative "I will never learn"?' Wherever they focus their attention, they will be reinforcing those 'brain connections' and neural networks.

The more we focus our attention on something, the stronger the neural connections will be. Consider playing the piano: the more we practise, the more focus and attention we give to the activity, the more our neurons fire, wire and reinforce those piano-playing neural connections, and we improve. As they say, practice makes perfect!

Interestingly, we now know from the research that the brain does not in fact differentiate 'real performance of an activity' from 'thought-only imaginary performance of an activity'.[1] This signifies that we can strengthen neural networks and even increase muscle strength only through the power of thought!

A 2004 study by Ranganathan et al.[2] involved one group performing 'little finger exercising' and another group just imagining they were exercising their little finger. Both performed their 'task' for the same number of minutes over the same period of time. The real performers increased their little finger muscle mass by 55%, which was to be expected. On the other hand, surprisingly, the 'thought only' group displayed an 35% augmentation of muscle mass! The power of thought![3]

Over the past ten years I have personally come to understand so much more about my own brain, and I am proud to say that I am now able to 'dominate' it. After childhood trauma reshaped my brain from the age of ten,[4] I believe I lived most of my life with my brain 'running on two different stories', as Bessel van der Kolk describes in his book *The Body*

---

[1] Pascual-Leone, A, Nguyet, D, Cohen, LG, Brasil-Neto, JP, Cammerota, A, & Hallet, M (1995). Modulation of muscle responses evoked by transcranial magnetic stimulation during the acquisition of new fine motor skills. *Journal of Neurophysiology, 74*(3), 1037–1045.

[2] Ranganathan, VK, Siemionow, V, Liu, JZ, Sahgal, V, & Yue, GH (2004). From mental power to muscle power: Gaining strength by using the mind. *Neuropsychologia, 42*(7), 944–956.

[3] For more information about the science behind visualisation and realisation see Pillay, S (2011). *The science behind the law of attraction: A step-by-step guide to putting the brain science behind the law of attraction to work for you*. NeuroBusiness Group.

[4] De Bellis, MD, & Zisk, A (2014). The biological effects of childhood trauma. *Child and Adolescent Psychiatric Clinics of North America, 23*(2), 185–222, vii. doi.org/10.1016/j.chc.2014.01.002

Keeps the Score.[5] All of my research over the past 15 years has led me to test many things for myself, leading to the calm reunification of my stories and an extremely calm and tranquil brain. I have finally been able to understand how to manage, optimise and maximise my brain capacity at a late stage in life.

One of my quests has been to help teachers to bring this knowledge to young learners and even adults. I wish I had grown up knowing how to manage my 'operating system'. For this reason, I would like to reach out to millions of you to help you understand your own brains and to understand the amazing holistic system, connecting brain, heart and gut, that we all carry within us.

There is a wonderful metaphor that originates from Tibetan Buddhist teachings: 'The brain is like a wild horse. You either learn to tame it, by sitting in that saddle and firmly taking the reins, or it will constantly gallop out of control, with you, the rider, running after it!' I spent most of my life galloping behind my own brain and emotions. How I wish to save others all those wasted years! Especially the children of today, who are also faced with the ever-increasing presence of AI and more advanced technologies in our lives!

Since the 1970s, modern neuroscience and neuropsychology have provided us with so many findings, as well as confirmation of previous psychological studies and practices such as meditation. The sophisticated evolution of modern technology through these years has offered us the amazing possibility of 'seeing' more about the brain and how the brain works. MRI research provides invaluable insights into brain structure and function.

However, one thing to bear in mind is that functional MRI (fMRI) does not measure actual neural activity. Instead, it tracks changes in blood flow (the BOLD signal, or blood oxygen level-dependent signal),[6]

---

[5] Van der Kolk, B (2014). *The body keeps the score: Brain, mind, and body in the healing of trauma.* Viking.

[6] Ogawa, S, Menon, RS, Kim, SG, & Ugurbil, K (1998). On the characteristics of functional magnetic resonance imaging of the human brain. *Proceedings of the National Academy of Sciences, 95*(3), 1486–1491. doi.org/10.1073/pnas.95.3.1486

which is assumed to correlate with brain activity. For this reason, there can never be a 100% foolproof guarantee to all the findings, and in addition neuroscience is an extremely progressive science which overturns itself – what we believe to be true today may be proven to be otherwise tomorrow!

Nevertheless, modern neuroscience is allowing us to demonstrate, reinforce and prove so many things we suspected or intuitively knew about our brains. Thanks to this, we are now able to grasp a deeper understanding of ourselves, as humans and, in our case, as educators.

The more that we as educators, trainers or coaches can bring this knowledge of the brain to our learners, the more effective their learning process is going to be. In fact, I personally believe we are well under way in an era of metacognition and neuroeducation, where our comprehension of the brain is key to more effective and efficient learning processes. Maybe even naively, I also believe that a deeper comprehension will lead to humanity communicating together in a totally different way and developing new ways of moving forward through this emergent new world in the twenty-first century.

We are living in times with huge question marks relating to education in general (and, having worked with teachers across the globe, this is a global phenomenon). Pre-pandemic education was struggling on many levels, but post-pandemic it has become even more alarmingly urgent to address new questions. For example, a surge in violence against educators suggests that both teachers and students are experiencing post-traumatic pandemic stress,[7] and accelerated brain ageing among adolescents due to pandemic isolation and stress raises graves concerns.[8] Just two of the serious issues that we are all faced with, not to mention the threatening emergence of advanced

---

[7] McMahon, SD, Martinez, A, & Espelage, DL (2024). Post-pandemic violence against educators: Understanding the surge and addressing PTSD. American Psychological Association Research Brief.

[8] Gotlib, IH, Walker, R, & Goodman, SH (2022). The adolescent brain in the pandemic: Accelerated aging and mental health. *Developmental Science, 26*(1), 102–118.

technologies and AI. To top it all, language teaching is one of the professions most at risk from these revolutionary technologies.[9]

Personally, I think a new era in education is rapidly emerging and many teachers across the globe are intuitively adopting new strategies to make their teaching effective. They must, to reach the learners!

Our educational systems have followed a one-size-fits-all approach that does not respect what we now know about the brain: that each brain is unique and different to any other brain.[10] While basic functioning may be the same, how we receive and interpret information may be significantly different to anyone else. I truly believe we are now shifting into a new style of transferring knowledge, where teachers are adapting to their learners. This will mean we need to rethink the group sizes of classes in schools or need to redesign learning activities and break groups into smaller study clusters. Additionally, we need to relieve teachers from burdensome administration and help them to spend more time developing the humane side of teaching – that is, the necessary human contact and deeper empathetic connection with the learner.

When famous Elon Musk took his children out of mainstream education and created his own school for them, it made me reflect. In an interview with Beijing TV in April 2015,[11] Musk said that his school 'does away with the traditional great structure of American primary education'. His goal in the new school was to cater for the skills of learners rather than force them to follow a set curriculum. I have also heard of many cases of children being taken out of school and given home tutoring, and this has often given excellent results, with children flourishing far more than they ever did at school.

---

[9] Felten, EW, Raj, M, & Seamans, R (2023). How will language modelers like ChatGPT affect occupations and industries? Available at SSRN: ssrn.com/abstract=4375268 or dx.doi.org/10.2139/ssrn.4375268

[10] Stern, P (2016). Every brain is different. *Science, 352*, 183. 0.1126/science.352.6282.183-b

[11] YouTube. 2015 Elon Musk on Ad Astra in California USA. youtube.com/watch?v=cXE5s-TzLCY

So, the real question for all educators nowadays is how we can adapt and improve to make learning more effective. Definitely, those of us who are adopting new ways and new styles of teaching delivery are recognising how our learners react differently. Not only do we now have access to key facts about the brain – how to change our brains, how to have healthy brains, and even how to optimise the performance of our brains – but we are also stepping up our understanding of social and emotional competences, intelligences, empathy and compassion. The 'neuro' prefix seems to be everywhere: neuroeconomics, neuromarketing, neuroculture, neurolaw and neuroleadership, to name just a few.

For me, the 'neuro' prefix has deep significance. Many people mistakenly only think of the brain when they hear it! In fact, it refers to neurons, and we have billions of neurons all over our bodies. In particular, the enteric nervous system (ENS), which is often referred to as the 'second brain', is estimated by some sources to include 500 million neurons.[12] And, of course, the heart possesses its own intrinsic nervous system, sometimes referred to as the 'heart's little brain.' In his research in 1991, Dr Armour detected that signals from the 'heart brain' redirect to the medulla, hypothalamus, thalamus, amygdala and cerebral cortex. Remarkably, the heart sends more signals to the brain than the other way round.[13]

This deeper significance of the 'neuro' means that we, as educators, can no longer treat learning as a 'brain-focused' process. Instead, we must bear in mind that learning may implicate a more holistic and deeper process taking place. Recent research even suggests that other cells in the body can learn and form memories too.[14]

---

[12] Mayer, EA (2011). Gut feelings: The emerging biology of gut-brain communication. *Nature Reviews Neuroscience, 12*(8), 453–466. doi.org/10.1038/nrn3071

[13] Alshami, AM (2019). Pain: Is it all in the brain or the heart? *Current Pain and Headache Reports, 23*(12), 88. doi.org/10.1007/s11916-019-0827-4

[14] Kukushkin, NV, Carney, RE, Tabassum, T et al. (2024). The massed-spaced learning effect in non-neural human cells. *Nature Communications, 15,* 9635. doi.org/10.1038/s41467-024-53922-x

As we gather more understanding of ourselves as humans, we are shifting into an era that will use all this information to optimise learning. Many schools are adopting new approaches imbued with emotional and social intelligence, mindfulness and metacognition as well as professional coaching and non-violent communication. These interweave in a beautifully calm framework that sets out a new way to dialogue with learners.

One outstanding foundation that has helped teachers to take a more 'neuro' approach for many years is the Hawn Foundation, founded by Goldie Hawn, which trains educators and children using MindUP™. This is their signature programme, which uses a brain-centric approach based on cognitive neuroscience, positive psychology and mindful awareness training. Ms Hawn herself talked about how she was 'always fascinated by the limitless potential of the brain' and how she has 'seen first-hand the positive impact of "heart-mind centric education" for children and educators'.[15] This positive impact is exactly what I have seen when people learn through the Neurolanguage Coaching approach, and all the certified Neurolanguage coaches worldwide are now witnessing this too.

In this book, I explain how Neurolanguage Coaching came about, what it consists of, how (in part) it is delivered and how a coachee can learn from this process. (Obviously a more guided and detailed version of this is delivered on our training courses!)

The phenomenon of language coaching, and Neurolanguage Coaching in particular, is currently storming the market (13 years after I started on this path!) because many language learners are now looking for something different and many corporations understand that their employees need a degree of English that will allow them to conduct business on a global scale. Today, more and more businesses are working across borders and more and more people need language skills that are adequate for business. This means that people need a

---

[15] From A Message from Goldie, a now-retired page of MindUP's website (accessed May 2016). For further information about the work of MindUP, see mindup.org

tailor-made, extremely personalised and more efficient way of learning languages. I propose that in the new age of AI, where more and more learners will regain their learner autonomy, there will be more of a need for the human coach teacher – the 'coacher'.

In the first part of this book, we will take a brief look at some of the landmarks in the development of language teaching and the current status of the language market, commenting on the types of teachers, trainers and coaches working with languages.

In the second part, we will talk about the development of neuroscience and the new era of neuro-learning, as well as introducing the underlying principles of neuroscience that are ever-pervasive in Neurolanguage Coaching.

Then, in the third part, we will move into the arena of professional coaching and language coaching/Neurolanguage Coaching. We will explore the differences between traditional language teaching and language coaching, as well as commenting on what Neurolanguage Coaching is not!

In the fourth part, we will go into the process and structure of Neurolanguage Coaching, examining the theoretical spiral learning process, the essential conversations and the structure of an engagement.

In part five, I will explain how to deliver grammar through brain-friendly coaching conversations, so that grammar becomes more fun to learn, as well as instantly graspable and applicable by the learner. (This was expanded in my second book, *Brain Friendly Grammar*, published in 2020 by Express Publishing.)[16]

As a reader, I hope to inspire you to start an inward journey into your own brain and how to learn languages, empowering you to know that we are all capable; it all depends on how we put our mind to the task.

If you are an educator, I hope to inspire you to initiate a deeper comprehension of how your own brain works in order to then transmit

---

[16] Paling, R (2020). *Brain-friendly grammar: Neurolanguage Coaching*®. Efficient Language Coaching Global SLU. ISBN: 9788409229048.

this information to your learner, giving you more insight into how to continually encourage, motivate and empower them. I also aim to inspire you to become much more metacognitively aware of how you teach and to empower you with professional coaching conversations that in turn unleash your learner's potential.

The following quotes highlight the eternal task of the Neurolanguage coach:

> *Tell me and I forget, teach me and I may remember, involve me and I learn.*

Benjamin Franklin beautifully encapsulates that a coaching approach is about opening a dialogue with our learners and involving them in the creation of their learning process. No more talking at learners, and much more talking with!

> *I am not a teacher, but an awakener.*

Robert Frost succinctly describes how educators are provoking neural connections leading to consolidation of knowledge. In Sanskrit, the word 'dheepa', meaning lamp or light, can be used together with 'vidya' – imparting knowledge – so 'vidya dheepa' symbolises a teacher who illuminates the path of knowledge.

In the end, language is about communication, and the more we can communicate with each other from the heart on a worldwide basis, the more we will be able to understand, appreciate and respect each other.

> *We, as human beings, learn through sharing and communicating.*

Hugo Reynolds

Part I

Part 1

Today's language market – still a thriving business worldwide

Over the past 20 years, language acquisition has been regarded as imperative. In such a globalised world, English is still definitely regarded as the major language, in particular for business, although now we see an emerging 'social media' English need too!

Other languages also have significant relevance and importance. In particular, Mandarin is spoken by approximately 1.2 billion native speakers and Spanish by 500 million native speakers in comparison to English, which is spoken by 400 million native speakers. However, English, as a native language and a second language, is in fact spoken by approximately 1.515 billion people.[17]

According to Global Market Insights,[18] the language learning market in 2023 was valued at approximately USD 61.5 billion and the English language learning market valued at USD 12.78 billion.[19]

Obviously, language learning is still central to educational systems worldwide and naturally forms a part of school curricula. Private individuals also may wish to increase their foreign language knowledge for personal reasons. Global business, wider geographical trade areas and, in addition, sophisticated modern technology all require the ability not only to converse in foreign languages but to master these to such a degree that business success may be guaranteed. Indeed, most companies today know that they are fighting within international

---

[17] Ethnologue (2024). What are the top 200 most spoken languages? ethnologue.com/insights/ethnologue200

[18] GMI (2024). Language learning market size. gminsights.com/industry-analysis/language-learning-market

[19] The Brainy Insights (2024). English language learning market size by end user. thebrainyinsights.com/report/english-language-learning-market-12711

arenas and expect their top executives to have a certain command over languages, in particular the English language. Interestingly, Jean-Paul Nerriére presented 'Globish' as a common-ground language that non-native English speakers could adopt in the context of international business.[20]

But is language learning still going to be required in the new era of AI? According to the British Council research 'The Future of English: Global Perspectives', the answer is a loud affirmative, but with an unexpected twist! It is recognised that the key role of English is as a 'tool underpinning and building "intercultural competence" rather than a foreign language' and there is a definite need for English in the use of social media and technology. The British Council recognise that teachers will still be central to the learning process, and therefore very much needed and in demand.

Another challenge today is how to motivate children within the educational system to learn more languages. It is interesting to note that many adult learners of language were greatly impacted, often negatively, by the language learning process in their childhood, and this, in fact, affects their mindset regarding the learning process as an adult in business. Constant exposure to the target language is imperative for the brain to become accustomed to doing business in a foreign language and to normalise this, so that the brain does not care whether it is using one language or another.

When we look at the language teaching industry, there is a full array of different types of language teachers. This ranges from school teachers within the educational system to certified and non- certified language teachers working privately or in the field of business. In fact, in the field of business I have encountered the range from the famous backpacker who dabbles in language classes for some extra cash to the extremely qualified and experienced language trainer; for example, back in the day I obtained a TEFL with ESP (English for Specific Purposes)

---

[20] Nerrière, JP, & Hon, D (2009). *Globish the world over*, vol. 1. St-Romain-en-Viennois: International Globish Institute.

qualification. Some even possess qualifications in a certain profession and have gone on to become specialised language consultants. For example, a qualified lawyer who delivers legal language training (this was also my case as I am a fully qualified non-practising UK lawyer!). One of the major questions in these cases is how to distinguish the quality and the experience of the trainer who is delivering such a service.

Over the last 20 years the phenomenon of language coaching has started to be heard, and more so over the last five years – in particular, in connection with business language teaching services. Many business English teachers, in fact, call themselves language coaches to distinguish themselves from other language teachers. The question as to what language coaching really is has become louder, and appears to have generated great confusion in the market.

In many ways, when I created the Neurolanguage Coaching approach and certification course back in 2012 (the pilot took place in 2012 and we went live in Paris in 2013), I could foresee this would happen. For me it was extremely important to enable language teachers to certify as 'recognised language coaches', thus serving as a benchmark for the market to recognise the certified, accredited and extremely experienced language trainers. Additionally, I wanted to arm these coaches with knowledge of the principles of neuroscience and how the brain likes to learn. This unique combination facilitates the delivery of language learning in a brain-friendly coaching style that flexibly adapts to each and every learner, no matter what age or background.

In my third book, Language Coaching in Action,[21] I endeavour to bring clarity by categorising different types of language coaches in the language learning market today. I do stress that there is no judgement of any of these and that it is up to our learners to decide which type of language coach they would like on their language learning journey.

---

[21] Paling, R (2023). *Language coaching in action: Brain-friendly materials using Neurolanguage Coaching.* Action Publishing Technology. ISBN: 9781789634181.

Here are the categorisations as quoted from the book:

> ➤ A language teacher who just uses the word 'coach' following the market trend and following the philosophy of the sports coach, with an empowering style and possibly an encouraging, empowering but potentially directive approach.

> ➤ A language teacher with many years of experience and expertise as such, who takes on the word 'coach' to demonstrate that experience. These are highly qualified language experts with an intuitively developed coaching style but normally no coaching training from an institution or body that standardises professional coaching.

> ➤ A language teacher who undertakes a life coaching qualification from an institution or body that certifies/accredits professional coaching training and then applies this knowledge to the language learning process. Here, there may be a grey line between life coaching and language learning and it may be necessary to really clarify with clients whether this is a 'life coaching' focus or a 'language coaching' focus.

> ➤ A language teacher who takes a language coaching course, which offers knowledge of the techniques and models from life coaching, using these to troubleshoot and enhance the learning process. These courses may carry certifications and CPDs (continuous professional development) for teachers but often are not accredited by an institution or body that standardises professional coaching.

> ➤ A language teacher who takes the Neurolanguage Coaching course,[22] which integrates professional coaching conversations, the coaching engagement structure, the essence of being a soundboard and a non-directive coach style together with the integration and the implementation of neuroscientific research, neuropsychology and emotional intelligence, which are all

---

[22] Neurolanguage Coaching. neurolanguagecoaching.com

interwoven into the language learning process as well as bringing metacognition to the learner. The course to become a Neurolanguage Coach is certified by Efficient Language Coaching and accredited by the International Coach Federation and also accredited by the UK Standards Office.

In my own experience working with corporates for over 15 years, companies expect English language expertise from many of their employees and often support them with in-house language learning programmes. However, companies through the years are continuously on a yo-yo of cost-cutting and expansion depending on company performance and expansion requirements. This means that many companies invest in language learning at dumping prices, so the quality of service given is not always the best and often does not achieve the required learning impact. Of course, this becomes the eternal dichotomy. Companies must cut costs and at the same time ensure quality learning that gives the company the necessary results for an effective globalised business.

Back in 2015, I remember going to a company interested in Neurolanguage Coaching for its employees. I had an excellent meeting with the HR director and explained the process and the profile of our team of coaches. He was highly impressed, but said he still had two other service providers to speak with. A week later he called me to say that the company management, although impacted by us as a new approach, had decided to go for an online learning platform that was (at that time) novel, 24-hour accessible by employees, fancy with its features and … of course … a lot cheaper! I was disappointed, to say the least!

One year later, he called me again. The online platform had failed – not because of the platform but because, after the initial honeymoon period, the employees had totally lost interest, so in the end they had paid for an annual contract but not achieved the results they had expected!

Companies searching for language services should fully understand the implications of such services and also check the qualifications of the language trainer, teacher or coach. If a language coach is sought, there should be evidence of some type of coaching qualification or they should be a certified and accredited Neurolanguage coach, who has received not only coach training but also training to implement neuroscientific principles, emotional intelligence and neuropsychology.

Human resources, or learning and development, should also collaborate with language coaches to create KPI measurements or measure learning progress through goal-setting programmes that entail regular reviews of those goals. Employees mostly struggle with the fluency of spoken language, so there should be great emphasis on training that helps employees to feel more comfortable and at ease when dealing in the target language, and especially for employees to understand how to manage nervousness or the activation of the sympathetic nervous system. It may be that quality training and coaching costs more, but in fact less time will be needed for the learning. So, effectively, in the long run, the company will be paying less!

As an additional comment, companies should bear in mind that no two brains are the same. Pushing learners into large groups will not only produce less effective learning, but could potentially harm some of those learners by causing increased embarrassment and discomfort when speaking the language. This means that a learner could potentially enter into a fight-or-flight mode[23] (activation of the sympathetic nervous system), and this in turn could shut down working memory capacity, attention and other prefrontal cortex functions.[24]

One of my corporate clients experienced exactly that! He was a brilliant C1 level in English, but in meetings he would shut down and start to stutter. We worked together to identify the emotional trigger

[23] First identified in animal behaviour by Walter Bradford Cannon, American physiologist.

[24] Ashcraft, MH (2002). Math anxiety: Personal, educational, and cognitive consequences. *Current Directions in Psychological Science, 11*(5), 181–185. doi.org/10.1111/1467-8721.00196

that was causing the stress and the shutdown and partnered to create coping strategies for him. After a few coaching sessions, he was able to manage by himself and within a short time was performing well in meetings![25] We will be looking at this in more depth in the next part of this book.

Over the next 20 years, language learning in companies may become more deeply integrated into business strategies, leveraging advanced technologies to make learning personalised, immersive and accessible. AI will play a significant role, as it tailors language learning experiences to individual employees' roles, industries and learning styles, providing instant real-time feedback. AI will also provide the 'any time, any place' convenience that is especially demanded by management and executives. Interactive AI-driven language tutors will be able to mimic real-life conversations, providing simulated workplace scenarios like meetings, negotiations and customer service interactions.

Nevertheless, I truly believe that global business success will embrace the importance of human connections and cultural understanding, and that the figure of the language coach will be the necessary human complement to the AI on offer.

---

[25] (a) Sandi, C, Pinelo-Nava, MT (2007). Stress and memory: Behavioral effects and neurobiological mechanisms. *Neural Plasticity*, e78970.
(b) Arnsten, AFT (1998). Enhanced: The biology of being frazzled. *Science, 280*(5370), 1711–1712.

Key developments in English language teaching

If we just take a moment to look back in time and highlight some key moments in English language teaching,[26] we can see that only last century did language teaching begin to emerge as a discipline and profession. Indeed, as Bill VanPatten rightly points out, 'before institutionalized education, language rules were non-existent. Pre-literate tribes world-wide learned other languages through contact without such rules. For example, there was contact among Native American tribes in North America long before Europeans came, and some tribal members learned another tribe's language … Phoenician was widely spoken as a second language in the ancient Mediterranean area, although no formal education system anywhere; there was no such thing as Phoenician 101.'[27]

In the seventeenth and eighteenth centuries, efforts to teach English to non-native speakers in colonial settings and among traders were mostly focused on the practicalities of trading and administration. Language learning was rooted in the study of classical languages like Latin and Greek. Institutionalisation can be traced to the 1750s, when English began to be taught in formal schools in colonial territories.

In 1946, the British Council took the decision to sponsor a journal called *English Language Teaching*, marking a pivotal moment for the professional development of English language teaching (ELT) in general. English language teaching qualifications and teacher training also became more formalised after a chair at the Institute of Education (University of London) was created in 1948.

---

[26] For a deeper history of English language teaching, please refer to Howatt, APR, with Widdowson, HG (2004). *A history of English language teaching*, 2nd ed. Oxford: Oxford University Press.

[27] VanPatten, B (2019). T*he nature of language*. ACTFL, 5.

The Association of Recognized English Language Schools (ARELS) was created in 1960 as a formal self-regulatory body, and later in 1967 the Association of Teachers of English as a Foreign Language (ATEFL) came into being, becoming IATEFL (with the addition of International, to reflect its international members) in 1971. In the US, the professional association called TESOL (Teaching English to Speakers of Other Languages) was founded in 1966 as a professional body to support English language educators worldwide. During the 1960s and 1970s, both ELT and applied linguistics flourished.

Interestingly from the Neurolanguage Coaching perspective, in the 1970s the 'communicative approach' (communicative language teaching, or CLT) emerged as a response to earlier methods, like the grammar-translation method and the audio-lingual method. Some believed that ELT was 'too technical and remote from the human concerns of teachers as well as learners'.[28] Earl W Stevick published articles and books between 1976 and 1990 to try to bring 'humanistic methods' back into language teaching.[29]

The primary goal of CLT was and is to develop communicative competence: the ability to use language effectively and appropriately in real-life situations, with an emphasis on interaction and communication over grammar and accuracy. Interestingly, we now know that the brain learns best with the real and personal![30] Research also suggests that we are more likely to remember information when we take it in socially.[31] I definitely would say that Neurolanguage Coaching is in line with this approach, through coaching conversations and the identification of the learner's focused goals.

---

[28] Howatt, APR, with Widdowson, HG (2004). *A history of English language teaching*, 2nd ed. Oxford: Oxford University Press, 255.

[29] For example, Stevick, EW (1976). *Memory, meaning & method: Some psychological perspectives on language learning*. Newbury House Publishers.

[30] Inter alia. Immordino-Yang, MH, & Damasio, AR (2007). We feel, therefore we learn: The relevance of affective and social neuroscience to education. *Mind, Brain, and Education*, 1(1), 3–10, and Davachi, L, Kiefer, T, Rock, D, & Rock, L (2010). Learning that lasts through AGES. *NeuroLeadership Journal*, 3, 53–63.

[31] Lieberman, MD (2013). *Social: Why our brains are wired to connect*. Oxford: Oxford University Press.

The communicative approach was mainly for adult learners and moved more towards specific needs learning, and this opened the doors for English for Specific Purposes (ESP). John Swales introduced genre analysis,[32] and this helped teachers to create more relevant materials for ESP learners. Needs analysis was and is central to ESP and is also central to the Neurolanguage Coaching process.

At this point it could be interesting to take a step back in time, prior to the communicative approach, to talk about the natural method (Sauveur) and the direct method (Berlitz) and also comment on these in relation to Neurolanguage Coaching.

I heartily concur with what John Locke wrote in 1693:[33]

> *Men learn languages for the ordinary intercourse of society and communication of thoughts in common life without any farther design in the use of them. And for this purpose, the original way of learning a language by conversation, not only serves well enough but is to be preferred as the most expedite, proper and natural.*

The natural method was developed by Lambert Sauveur in the late 1870s, and I really like the way he gave his invaluable advice on how to talk to learners in his work *An Introduction to the Teaching of Living Languages Without Grammar or Dictionary.*[34] He said that there are two basic principles. The first was only to ask 'earnest questions', and the second was 'to connect scrupulously the questions in such a manner that one may give rise to another'. Reflecting upon these words, we see the precursors for powerful questions in professional coaching and in Neurolanguage Coaching. Provocative questions are key to facilitating critical thinking and helping the learner to assimilate new language.

---

[32] Swales, JM (1990). *Genre analysis: English in academic and research settings.* Cambridge: Cambridge University Press.

[33] From John Locke's open letter titled Some Thoughts Concerning Education, now widely available online.

[34] Howatt, APR, with Widdowson, HG (2004). *A history of English language teaching*, 2nd ed. Oxford: Oxford University Press, 218–221.

In the latter part of the nineteenth century, the direct method emerged. Apparently, Maximilian Berlitz, an immigrant in the USA, founded the language centre Berlitz in 1878. He hired Nicholas Joly as a French instructor, but discovered he could not speak a word of English. As Berlitz was ill when Joly arrived, Joly delivered the French as best he could! When Berlitz returned, he was astounded that his students were speaking French well, with good pronunciation and grammar. This inspired him to create the Berlitz method, or direct method, with the philosophy that, from the first moment on, learners should only be exposed to the target language.

However, this is in fact a point on which Neurolanguage Coaching differs from the Berlitz method. Yes, I agree with as much exposure to the target language as possible; however, teaching beginners in the target language only could trigger a fight-or-flight response and in fact hinder the learning. We will talk more about this in part II.

In addition, I am a firm believer in learning by association, due to my own language learning experience. The more the learner's brain can associate and make connections between native and target language, the greater the 'aha' effect and the faster the learning.

On the other hand, I am not saying that the native language should be continuously spoken. Not at all! I strongly believe that constantly exposing the brain to the target language is extremely beneficial and aids the learning process. What I am saying is that there should be the freedom to use the native language, and also to explain whenever necessary in the native language, so that the emotional brain remains calm.

As another example of native versus target language, Harold E Palmer, who developed the oral method in the 1920s, excluded teaching grammar in the students' native language because he believed that grammatical rules should come through 'habit formation'.[35]

As previously mentioned, I agree with this! I have witnessed that my own learners do make connections when we ask them to reflect upon

---

[35] Palmer, HE (1921). *The principles of language-study*. New York: World Book Company.

the similarities or dissimilarities of the grammar with known native structures (rather than take them through the grammar rules!). Interestingly, research led by Kirsten Weber at the Max Planck Institute in Nijmegen tells us: 'Processing a known structure is easier for the brain second time round. As a whole, our study shows that we seem to use the same brain areas for native and new language structures and that "Alienese" was in the process of being integrated into the participants' existing language brain networks.'[36] (Participants were taught an 'alien language' which had elements of new structures and similarities to native structures.)

Another method worth highlighting is the natural approach by Stephen Krashen and Tracy Terrell.[37] This approach is based on the idea that language acquisition is most effective when it mirrors the natural process of first language learning. In this approach, language learning happens through comprehensible input: that is, language that is just above the current proficiency level of the learner but still understandable. This method emphasises communication, immersion, and the use of real-world language rather than explicit grammar instruction. Krashen's theories regarding acquisition learning and the affective filter reflect how the brain learns and how it may be affected by stress or social pain. I talk more about this in relation to the activation of the sympathetic nervous system in part II.

Another approach that developed from the communicative approach was the Dogme language teaching movement introduced by Scott Thornbury in 2000 (though the ideas were being discussed in the mid-1990s). The key idea behind Dogme is a focus on conversation-driven teaching, with a strong emphasis on authentic communication and learner-centred approaches. It advocates for minimising the use of pre-planned materials (like textbooks) and encourages teachers to create

---

[36] Weber, K, Christiansen, MK, Petersson, KM, Indefrey, P, & Hagoort, P (2016). fMRI syntactic and lexical repetition effects reveal the initial stages of learning a new language. *Journal of Neuroscience, 36*(26), 6872–6880.

[37] Krashen, S, & Terrell, T (1983). *The natural approach: Language acquisition in the classroom.* Oxford: Pergamon Press.

lessons that emerge from the learners' needs and interests in real-time. The emphasis is on real communication, learner autonomy, and meaningful interaction in the classroom. Thornbury suggests that language teaching should be material-light and conversation-heavy.[38]

In this respect, Neurolanguage Coaching is very much in line with the Dogme approach and expands on this through the use of professional coaching conversations plus the integration of the 'neuro' aspects.

If we really looked deeply into the development of language learning throughout the last century, we could witness a constant push and pull between the traditional methods such as grammar translation and the more progressive methods such as the communicative approach. In addition, as in all disciplines, some methods or approaches have been more in favour at a given time due to the influential parties steering such trends. Now, I would suggest, as we move further into the twenty-first century, the question is how to integrate all the wisdom gained from the past to facilitate, wherever possible, the faster and more efficient learning process necessary for the world and especially the learners of today. Additionally, such a learning process should follow the principles that we now know concerning how the brain functions, connects and learns and – most importantly – should respect the fact that every brain is unique.

From this perspective, Neurolanguage Coaching is deeply rooted in self-determination theory (SDT)[39] and learner autonomy (LA).[40]

SDT focuses on human motivation and personality development. It emphasises the importance of intrinsic motivation and lays out three basic psychological needs for individuals to experience optimal motivation and wellbeing: the need to feel in control of one's actions and decisions (autonomy), the need to feel capable and effective in

---

[38] Thornbury, S (2000). *Teaching unplugged: Dogme in English language teaching.* In *English Teaching Professional, 18,* 3–8.

[39] Deci, EL, & Ryan, RM (1985). *Intrinsic motivation and self-determination in human behavior.* Springer Science & Business Media.

[40] Holec, H (1981). *Autonomy and foreign language learning.* Oxford: Pergamon.

performing tasks (competence), and the need to feel connected to others and experience a sense of belonging (relatedness). In learning, supporting autonomy and competence can lead to better learning outcomes, increased motivation, and greater personal growth.

The term 'learner autonomy' (Henri Holec) refers to learners taking control of their own learning process, allowing them to choose learning content, pace and strategies. Learners are empowered to set their own learning goals, look for their own resources, monitor and evaluate progress and learning. In this way learners become active participants in their learning, rather than passive recipients of information.

In summary, Neurolanguage Coaching embraces elements of all methods and approaches and centres upon the unique learner, who can then decide the learning approach that suits them best. It offers a framework that adapts and personalises the process, tailoring it to the individual or the group.

As a final note to this part, Howatt and Widdowson[41] talk about learning a language through constant conversation. They state that:

> ... *learning how to speak a new language, it is held, is not a rational process which can be organised in a step- by-step manner following graded syllabuses of new points to learn, exercises and explanations. It is an intuitive process for which human beings have a natural capacity that can be awakened provided only that the proper conditions exist.*

And this awakening is exactly what Neurolanguage Coaching aspires to achieve.

---

[41] Howatt, APR, with Widdowson, HG (2004). *A history of English language teaching*, 2nd ed. Oxford: Oxford University Press, 210.

Part II

Over 50 years of neuroscience

I distinctly remember that phone call back in 2015! John (not his real name) was interested in doing my ELC Language Coaching certification course, and we were talking about the content of the course. He was working at a university in Germany at the time.

When it got to the neuroscience, he asked me, 'Why do you have neuroscience in this course?' and I explained that it was to bring more light onto how the brain learns, functions and reacts. He replied, 'But we never did this before as teachers,' and my gut reply was, *And isn't it time that we did?*

Over 50 years of neuroscience and still we are struggling to apply the knowledge in education. One of the major problems is the bridge between the theory and the practice. The underlying dilemma is how to 'embody' the research and the information that we now have about our brains!

As I mentioned in the introduction, neuroscience is not limited to the brain. It is about the holistic functioning of brain, heart and gut in unison, as well as the central and peripheral nervous systems. As an example of this holistic connection, scientists are researching how Parkinson's disease is linked to gut bacteria![42].

So how do we integrate the 'neuro' into Neurolanguage Coaching? We do this from three perspectives.

Firstly, we talk about the brain with our learners according to their needs, with the goal of optimising their learning. This discussion could relate to how we function, how we learn and how we react. One of the major functions of our brain is 'to understand' and, by opening up

---

[42] Sampson, TR, Debelius, JW, Thron, T, Janssen, S, Shastri, GG, et al. (2016). Gut microbiota regulate motor deficits and neuroinflammation in a model of Parkinson's disease. *Cell, 167*(6), 1469–1480.

these dialogues, we help our learners to understand themselves better. This leads to more metacognition or self-awareness.

Secondly, we integrate the findings of neuroscientific research into the process, so that most of what we do relates back to the research. For example, the principle of chunking down[43] and spacing out,[44] the flow state,[45] provocation of connections through scaffolding, inter alia.

Thirdly, we communicate in a very brain-friendly manner, to ensure a relaxed learning process.

This will contribute to the learner maintaining a 'calm brain'.

Back in the 1990s, Caine and Caine[46] outlined key principles of brain-based learning, including how brain research can inform effective teaching strategies. They offered a framework for making learning more aligned with the brain's natural ways of processing information. Some of the foundational concepts that they introduced are:

- ➤ The brain is a parallel processor.

- ➤ Learning engages the entire physiology.

- ➤ The search for meaning is innate and occurs through patterning.

- ➤ Emotions are critical to patterning.

- ➤ The brain processes wholes and parts simultaneously. Although

---

[43] Christiansen, MH, & Chater, N (2016). The now-or-never bottleneck: A fundamental constraint on language. *Behavioral and Brain Sciences, 39*, e62.
doi.org/10.1017/S0140525X16000637

[44] Kapler, I, Weston, T, & Wiseheart, M (2015). Spacing in a simulated undergraduate classroom: Long-term benefits for factual and higher-level learning. *Learning and Instruction, 36*. 10.1016/j.learninstruc.2014.11.001.

[45] Egbert, J (2004). A study of flow theory in the foreign language classroom. *Canadian Modern Language Review, 60*(5), 549–586.
utppublishing.com/doi/abs/10.3138/cmlr.60.5.549

[46] Caine, RN, & Caine G (1998). *Making connections: Teaching and the human brain.* Association for Supervision and Curriculum Development, and Caine, RN, & Caine, G (2000). *The brain-targeted teaching model for 21st-century schools.* Corwin Press.

there are differences between right and left hemispheres in terms of their functions, there is a certain integrity between the two hemispheres.

➤ Learning involves both focused attention and peripheral perception.

➤ Learning involves both conscious and unconscious processes. We learn much more than what we understand consciously.

➤ We have two types of memory. These are spatial and mechanical learning systems.

➤ We understand and remember best when facts and skills are embedded in natural, spatial memory.

➤ Experienced-based learnings are the best ways to use spatial memory.

➤ Learning is enhanced by challenge and inhibited by threat.

➤ Each brain is unique.

I find it hard to believe that their work is over 25 years old and we are still not fully integrating this knowledge into teacher training programmes across the world!

Since I started delivering my courses back in 2013, my quest has been to bring this knowledge to teachers. Through these years, I have realised that many teachers are in fact intimidated and frightened by this knowledge, and that is the reason that it has to be delivered to them in a very simplified and easy-to-understand manner. Most importantly, the teachers in turn have to be able to pass this knowledge to their learners. Therefore, they need to build confidence in sharing information about the brain.

And let's go back to John! Why talk about the brain? What is the effectiveness of talking about metacognition in schools?

In fact, the impact is great![47] Teaching metacognitive strategies can have a positive impact on students' learning outcomes. Metacognition, or thinking about one's own thinking, is associated with better performance and more positive motivation cycles. A growth mindset also impacts learners,[48] and 'neuroscience intervention' can lead to students planning in a more organised fashion as well as more self-reliance and self-confidence.[49]

Through these 13 years, I have seen how teachers transform on my course as they come to understand more about their own minds, and I have heard many testimonials from their learners, impacted by the information transmitted by their coaches. One of our teacher trainers told me how she had explained fight-or-flight to her five-year-old. As a family they were due to emigrate back to Japan from Belgium, and the little boy was experiencing panic attacks. She simplified the explanation into baby language and explained that his brain was 'trying to protect him' and that, if he felt at any time that his brain was 'not happy', he should tell her and together they would do something to calm the brain down. She told me how effective that conversation had been, because he would come and find her, saying, 'Mummy, mummy, my brain is starting again!'

So, on the course, we take a step-by-step crescendo approach to the brain and how it functions, reacts and learns. We look at neurons, at how they connect, and at neuroplasticity. We look at pruning and memory. How we learn as children and as adults, together with brainwaves and the different 'brain states'. We look at key areas in the

[47] Perry, J, Lundie, D, & Golder, G (2019). Metacognition in schools: What does the literature suggest about the effectiveness of teaching metacognition in schools? *Educational Review, 71*(4), 483–500. doi.org/10.1080/00131911.2018.1441127

[48] Blackwell, L, Trzesniewski, K, & Dweck, C (2007). Implicit theories of intelligence predict achievement across an adolescent transition: A longitudinal study and an intervention. *Child Development, 78*(1), 246–263. doi.org/10.1111/j.1467-8624.2007.00995.x

[49] Cherrier, S, Le Roux, PY, Gerard, FM, Wattelez, G, & Galy, O (2020). Impact of a neuroscience intervention (NeuroStratE) on the school performance of high school students: Academic achievement, selfknowledge and autonomy through a metacognitive approach. *Trends in Neuroscience and Education, 18*, 100125.

brain that are impacted by emotional triggers, and how the activation of the sympathetic nervous system can block and hinder learning. We learn how to coach around emotional triggers. Then we explore the factors that contribute to what I call a 'perfect learning state'. This leads into explicit and implicit learning as well as 'the learning journey' and the flow state. We explore the neuromyth around learning styles and how to coach learners around their preferred ways of learning. Finally, we conclude the neuroscience part of the course by exploring language comparisons more deeply to provoke connections. All of this forms the pervasive 'neuro' element in Neurolanguage Coaching.

In the next part of this book, I will focus more deeply on the seven key underlying neuroscientific principles in the Neurolanguage process.

Firstly, let us break down and simplify neuroscience to introduce some important aspects. According to the online Cambridge dictionary, neuroscience is the scientific study of the nervous system and the brain.[50] From a broader perspective, we can understand that this includes all aspects of the nervous system: its structure, function and development, and its role in behaviour and cognition. In addition, it incorporates knowledge from diverse disciplines, such as psychology, medicine and physics.

Educational neuroscience and neuroeducation are particularly interesting in relation to learning. The former studies how the brain learns and how neuroscience findings can help to shape educational practices. The latter integrates neuroscience, psychology and education to create practical teaching strategies and tools.

In one of the critiques of the first edition of this book, I was accused of confusing the brain and the mind! It is true to say that I did not draw a distinction between the physical brain and the abstract mind, and indeed the mind arises from the brain's activities. But for me, they are not disjointed and do not need to be separated out, as they operate as one 'operating system'. It is nearly impossible to talk about one without

---

[50] Cambridge Dictionary. Neuroscience. dictionary.cambridge.org/dictionary/english/neuroscience

referencing the other, especially when discussing learning, cognition or behaviour.

When using the computer metaphor, many talk about the brain being the hardware and the mind the software. For example, learning involves physical changes in the brain, such as the strengthening or weakening of neural connections. The mind interprets and makes meaning of what is learned. Emotions, motivation and subjective experiences (e.g. the joy of discovery) are key drivers of learning.

The brain comprises almost 100 billion neurons and even more non-neuronal cells according to the latest research, which also identified approximately 3,313 different cell types in the brain![51] There are also up to a trillion synaptic connections. Neurons communicate directly with one another, sending messages in the form of electrochemical signals or electrical impulses (action potentials), but they do not actually physically touch each other as they communicate with each other across a synaptic gap. This gap is about 20 to 40 nanometres wide;[52] I never cease to be amazed when I try to imagine this.

In very simple terms, cell-to-cell communication occurs when an action potential travels down a neuron to the synaptic gap to connect with other neurons or other cells. This is very nicely expressed by Hebb's law, which states that 'cells that fire together wire together'.[53]

Whenever there is brain activity, there can be millions of neurons firing together at the same time. This firing produces electrical activity, which can be measured or monitored by an electroencephalogram, or EEG for short. Multiple electrodes are placed along the scalp and the EEG measures the voltage fluctuations.

Neurons connect to create incredibly vast and intricate neural networks. Our neural networks or maps are in fact our personal

---

[51] Weninger, A, & Arlotta, P (2023). A family portrait of human brain cells. *Science, 382,* 168–9. doi.org/10.1126/science.adk4857

[52] Kandel, ER, Schwartz, JH, & Jessell, TM (2012). *Principles of neural science,* 5th ed. McGraw-Hill.

[53] Hebb, DO (1949). *The organization of behavior.* New York: Wiley.

internal representations of the external world. Interestingly, wherever we focus our attention and energy, those brain maps will become more ingrained or embedded into long-term memory.

Just as an additional note, we shouldn't forget in this simplified overview that there are many other cells in the brain besides neurons that have important functions. For example, glial cells, particularly astrocytes, play a role in synaptic plasticity and learning.[54]

One of the greatest breakthroughs with regard to neuromyths about the brain is the realisation that the brain is in fact plastic and not static, meaning that the brain can remodel and remap its connections. Back in the seventies and eighties, some brave neuroscientists defied the theory that the brain was static! One of these was Michael Merzenich, whose work proved that the brain retains its ability to change well into adulthood.

Neuroplasticity is the ability of the brain and nervous system to change structurally and functionally in response to its experience. By learning new things and having new experiences, the brain starts to embed new patterns of neural networks, thus reshaping itself.

Over the last 50 years, there has been a lot of research relating to neuroplasticity, and some amazing results. For example, studies on how meditation reshapes the brain. One study shows that, after six to eight weeks of regular meditation, the prefrontal cortex becomes thicker and the amygdala shrinks.[55] Meanwhile, London taxi drivers were shown to have an increase of grey matter in the hippocampal region (related to spatial navigation) due to years and years of 'mapping' the streets of London in their brains.[56]

---

[54] Allen, N, Barres, B (2009). Glia – more than just brain glue. *Nature, 457*, 675–677. doi.org/10.1038/457675a

[55] Taren, AA, Creswell, D, & Gianaros, PJ (2013). Dispositional mindfulness co-varies with smaller amygdala and caudate volumes in community adults. *PLOS ONE, 8*(5), e64571.

[56] Maguire, EA, Woollett, K, & Spiers, HJ (2006). London taxi drivers and bus drivers: A structural MRI and neuropsychological analysis. *Hippocampus, 16*(12), 1091–1101. doi.org/10.1002/hipo.20233

Even though we have all the research and proof of neuroplasticity, I do think that we are not living and embodying it enough! I still hear learners saying 'I am too old to learn' or 'I will never be able to learn that'.

I also think we need to change societal judgements relating to age. On the one hand, we need to explain to children that when they leave school, they do not need to know what they want to do for the rest of their life! We need to broaden their perspectives by explaining they can change professions throughout their lives and that lifelong learning is key.[57] When I was at university in my early thirties studying law, I met a lady who was in her late thirties studying to become a doctor. This was her third degree! Her first after school was in theology. Later, in her late twenties, she had studied law and became a UK barrister, and at this point in her life she was going through med school! She qualified in her mid-forties and is now practising as a GP in the UK. What an amazing role model!

On the other hand, we should also change our judgements about retirement. I would actually propose to rename it 'recalibration'! Research about 'superagers' – that is, people in their nineties with the most amazing brains – concludes that the three elements that help us become superagers are physical exercise, mental exercise and positive social connections.[58]

As educators, I think we need to encourage children and adults of all ages to really embrace neuroplasticity and how we can change our brains!

Another amazing breakthrough happened in 1998 when scientists discovered that, contrary to previous beliefs, the human brain

---

[57] Ates, H, & Alsal, K (2012). The importance of lifelong learning has been increasing. *Procedia – Social and Behavioral Sciences*, *46*(12), 4092–4096.
10.1016/j.sbspro.2012.06.205

[58] Cook, A, Kielb, S, Loyer, E, Connelley, M, Rademaker, A, Mesulam, MM, Weintraub, S, McAdams, D, Logan, R, & Rogalski, E (2017). Psychological well-being in elderly adults with extraordinary episodic memory. *PLOS ONE*, *12*(10), e0186413.
10.1371/journal.pone.0186413

produces new nerve cells into adulthood.[59] This gave us clear evidence of neurogenesis, the creation of new neurons, thus breaking down the neuromyth that adults were not able to produce new brain cells. Now we know we do!

In 2016, research also demonstrated that after a certain period of aerobic exercise, the generation of neurons kicks in.[60] This neurogenesis is seen to occur in the hippocampal region, an area that is important for spatial and episodic memory. More research not only concurs with exercise's promotion of neurogenesis, but also demonstrates that regular exercise improves memory and cognition and that, on top of that, just 20 minutes of moderate exercise improves attention for up to two hours after.[61] I often joke that we should ask our learners to exercise for 20 minutes before starting a learning session with us!

With a basic understanding of:

➤ how neurons connect

➤ how the brain is plastic and can change and develop

➤ how neurogenesis is possible

we can encourage the change in mindset towards lifelong learning and really encourage learners of any age. This is particularly necessary when a learner has a negative mindset towards learning at a later stage in life. We now know that we can learn and achieve the most amazing things at any age.

---

[59] Gage, FH, & Kempermann, G (1999). New neural cells for the adult brain. *Scientific American*, *28*(5), 48–53.

[60] Nokia, MS, Lensu, S, Ahtiainen, JP, Johansson, PP, Koch, LG, Britton, SL, & Kainulainen, SL (2016). Physical exercise increases adult hippocampal neurogenesis in male rats provided it is aerobic and sustained. *Journal of Physiology*, *594*(7), 1855–1873.

[61] Basso, JC, & Suzuki, WA (2017). The effects of acute exercise on mood, cognition, neurophysiology, and neurochemical pathways: A review. *Brain Plasticity*, *2*(2), 127–152. doi.org/10.3233/BPL-160040

In addition, it is essential to understand that every brain is different![62] No two people have the same brain anatomy, as proven by researchers at the University of Zurich.[63]

Some scientists say that we genetically inherit about 50% of our neural networks and the other 50% consists of the input of our own knowledge and experiences throughout life. Others say only one third is genetic and two thirds are our own input. In any case, the amazing fact is that whatever I have as my genetic makeup plus all the knowledge that I possess in my brain is absolutely unique to me, just as your genetic makeup and whatever you have engrained in your brain – whether through learning, environmental exposure, life experience or whatever – is unique to you. This also means that each and every one of us will perceive, receive and interpret information in different ways!

> The crucial point to remember when we, as educators, are together with our learner or learners is that:
>
> ➤ each learner's brain is unique.

It is interesting and important to understand some of the key brain areas crucial to the learning process. Obviously, the brain in its entirety is important – metaphorically speaking, all instruments in an orchestra have a definite role – but there are some key areas which will afford a better understanding of Neurolanguage concepts, namely the calm brain approach.

The first area to highlight is the cerebellum, which plays an important role in motor control, and prior to the 1990s was believed to be purely

[62] Stern, P (2016). Every brain is different. *Science, 352*, 183. 10.1126/science.352.6282.183-b

[63] Valizadeh, SA, Liem, F, Mérillat, S, Hänggi, J, & Jäncke, L (2018). Identification of individual subjects on the basis of their brain anatomical features. *Scientific Reports, 8*(1), 5611. doi.org/10.1038/s41598-018-23696-6

motor-related. Research shows it is also active regarding language, attention and mental imagery.[64] Studies show that there are interactions between the cerebellum and other areas of the cerebral cortex, which is the outer covering of grey matter over the hemispheres.

There is speculation as to whether the cerebellum is also part of the unconscious mind which learns, remembers and stores actions and responses in particular from early childhood. It is crucial for procedural memory, which governs the learning of habits and motor skills. The cerebellum contains

more than half of all the neurons in the human brain. In 2017, it was shown to play an important role as part of a broader language network, specifically in tasks related to verbal fluency.[65] More recent research suggests that the cerebellum should be considered a key component of the brain's language system.[66]

Now, in very simple terms, it can be suggested that language production is a front-to-back coordinated operation across the brain! In the left frontal lobe, the famous Broca's area manages speech production, syntax and articulation. The prefrontal cortex manages working memory during speech production. Wernicke's area in the left temporal lobe manages language comprehension and the meanings of words. The angular gyrus and supramarginal gyrus in the parietal lobe contribute to language processing. Then at the back we have the cerebellum and its role in verbal fluency, assisting with motor coordination by fine-tuning speech production and supporting cognitive processing.

---

[64] Marien, P, Ackermann, H, Adamszek, M, Barwood, CHS, Beaton, A, et al. (2014). Consensus paper: Language and the cerebellum: An ongoing enigma. *Cerebellum, 13*(3), 386–410.

[65] Vias, C, & Dick, AS (2017). Cerebellar contributions to language in typical and atypical development: A review. *Developmental Neuropsychology, 42*(6), 404–421. doi.org/10.1080/87565641.2017.1334783

[66] LeBel, A, & D'Mello, AM (2023). A seat at the (language) table: Incorporating the cerebellum into frameworks for language processing. *Current Opinion in Behavioral Sciences, 53*, 101310, ISSN 2352-1546. doi.org/10.1016/j.cobeha.2023.101310

When we are communicating naturally, this front-to-back/back-to-front flow of language is fluid. Now just imagine that there is an emotional trigger. In my mind, the mid-brain or limbic region represents a gate that blocks that flow. Even in our native language, we all know that feeling of becoming tongue-tied or muted in moments of stress or pressure.

If we stay in that mid-brain region, the next area to highlight is the hippocampus, which has a major role in learning and memory.[67]

I describe the hippocampus as a memory 'organiser' and 'encoder'; some have criticised me for that, but there is a general consensus in the research that it is indeed involved in converting short- term memories to long-term ones. It decides what should be stored in short-term memory and in long-term memory. It is also important for spatial navigation.

Cleveland Clinic website states: 'The hippocampus converts short-term memories into long-term memories by organizing, storing and retrieving memories within your brain. Your hippocampus also helps you learn more about your environment (spatial memory), so you're aware of what's around you, as well as remembering what words to say (verbal memory).'[68]

Obviously, the hippocampus is one of the essential components for learning as it is one of the 'deciders' for memory encoding in the brain. Therefore, when learning, we need this area of the brain to be fully functional. If we have a learner in a fight-or-flight response, this may result in the temporary inhibition of hippocampal activity.

We move now to the prefrontal cortex (PFC), which is the portion of the cerebral cortex that covers the front part of the frontal lobe of the brain. It is responsible for higher cognitive functions, or our 'executive

[67] Anand, KS, & Dhikav, V (2012). Hippocampus in health and disease: An overview. *Annals of Indian Academy of Neurology*, 15(4), 239-46. doi.org/10.4103/0972-2327.104323

[68] Cleveland Clinic, Hippocampus. my.clevelandclinic.org/health/body/hippocampus

functions'.[69] Analysing, creating, planning, learning, remembering, making decisions, emotional regulation, and even visualising all take place in this part of the brain. It is the part that is the most active when we are consciously concentrating and plays a key role in working memory. When learning we need the PFC to be fully operative; the fight-or-flight mode would prevent rational, logical thought or learning as our survival mode would kick in.

Finally, to bring full attention to the fight-or-flight mode and the activation of the sympathetic nervous system, it is essential to mention the amygdala.

The amygdala is part of the mid-brain or the limbic regions and, in simple terms, could be described as responsible for triggering the alarm whenever a survival question arises. It's fascinating to think that, in fact, a part of our brain is constantly scanning and checking that we are 'safe' and out of 'danger', and the amygdala forms part of the mechanism that immediately alerts the body to any threat situation. Interestingly, the amygdala will also create certain emotions like rage to protect us in life-threatening situations.

In his book *Emotional Intelligence*,[70] Daniel Goleman refers to the amygdala hijack, where our emotions can override the conscious brain, leading us to emotional reactions that we may not rationally understand. When the alarm is triggered, urgent messages are sent to every major part of the brain. The body's fight-or-flight mechanisms[71] start to mobilise.

We all know those telltale signs when the sympathetic nervous system is activated as a physiological response to a threat. Namely, quickened heart rate, raised blood pressure, rapid breathing, shaking, blurred vision and unclear thoughts.

---

[69] Miller, E, & Cohen, J (2001). An integrative theory of prefrontal cortex function. *Annual Review of Neuroscience*, 24, 167–202. 10.1146/annurev.neuro.24.1.167

[70] Goleman, D (1995). *Emotional intelligence*. London: Bloomsbury.

[71] First described in Cannon, WB (1929). *Bodily changes in pain, hunger, fear, and rage*. New York: Appleton-Century-Crofts.

At this point, the body, preparing for fight or flight, directs blood away from the visceral organs of the body into the arms and legs, enabling either the 'stay and fight' scenario or the 'run away fast' scenario. Blood flow and neural activity are focused on survival rather than higher-order cognitive processes. Therefore, conscious and rational thought moves to the back of the queue, because in this survival mode we really do not have the time to hang around debating if we should fight or run! So the two major areas needed for the learning process, the prefrontal cortex and the hippocampus, are both impacted.[72]

Nowadays, we are constantly exposed to situations that can be perceived as a threat by our brain (such as delivering a presentation in a foreign language!). We also now know from research that when we experience social pain, our brain does in fact activate neural regions associated with physical pain.[73] So, in effect, the brain registers social pain in the same area of the brain and almost to the same degree as it does for physical pain. In short, we know that life-threatening situations trigger the amygdala and 'limbic reactions', and we also know that social pain and emotional pain can also trigger the same reactions to a lesser or greater degree.

A nice example of some 'amygdala arousers' can be found in the SCARF model by David Rock.[74] This model illustrates five domains of human social experience which could trigger the fight-or-flight response in a given situation.

---

[72] (a) Sandi, C, & Pinelo-Nava, MT (2007). Stress and memory: Behavioral effects and neurobiological mechanisms. *Neural Plasticity*, e78970.
(b) Phelps, EA (2006). Emotion and cognition: Insights from studies of the human amygdala. *Annual Review of Psychology*, *57*, 27–53.
(c) Arnsten, AFT (1998). Enhanced: The biology of being frazzled. *Science*, *280*(5370), 1711–1712.

[73] Eisenberger, NI (2012). The neural bases of social pain: Evidence for shared representations with physical pain. *Psychosomatic Medicine*, *74*(2), 126–135.

[74] SCARF is an acronym of the social concerns that drive human behaviour: status, certainty, autonomy, relatedness and fairness. See Rock, D (2008). SCARF: A brain-based model for collaborating with and influencing others. *Neuroleadership Journal*, *1*(1), 44.

Let us now imagine a scenario where speaking a foreign language triggers the brain into that feeling of being in a life-threatening situation. The survival mechanism kicks in and conscious rational thought processes no longer flow, impacting and compromising the PFC executive functions and hippocampal memory formation. In this way, the learner feels totally blocked and closed to the learning process, and in essence this block is actually real, due to the way the fight-or-flight response limits resources to the areas needed for learning.

Indeed, learning a language could trigger all types of negative reactions: typically, shame and embarrassment as well as feelings of uncertainty, inadequacy and frustration. There is even the phenomenon of foreign language anxiety or xenoglossophobia in three main areas:[75] communication apprehension, test anxiety and fear of negative evaluation.

As Neurolanguage coaches we are fully trained to explain the fight-or-flight response to our learners, as well as to coach them around any emotional triggers that may arise during the learning process.

The teacher, trainer and coach should be:

➤ able to fully understand the key roles of the cerebellum, hippocampus and prefrontal cortex in the learning process.

➤ aware of the amygdala and limbic system reactions to potential threat.

➤ extremely empathetic to any type of social or emotional pain or foreign language anxiety in a learner, as this triggered reaction could impact and impede the learning process.

➤ able to coach the learner around the perceived threat situation, so that the brain can return to its normal calm and unthreatened state.

Now, I would like to briefly touch upon how we learn. From pre-birth to age seven, the brain is constantly absorbing brand new information

---

[75] Horwitz, EK, Horwitz, MB, & Cope, J (1986). Foreign language classroom anxiety. *Modern Language Journal*, 70(2), 125–132.

and constantly making new neural connections. In particular, at this age we are forging subconscious programmes that provide us with the foundational basis to function and survive. For example, walking, talking, getting dressed, washing etc. all become 'automated processes'.

Obviously, a child's brain has amazing plasticity, capable of surprising achievements such as becoming bilingual or multilingual at early ages. From the age of six, our brains seemingly shift from predominant subconscious mind into a 'calm consciousness'.[76] Those early years are heavily influenced by implicit learning (procedural memory), and from six to seven onwards the PFC becomes more involved in decision-making, planning and attention control. However, the PFC is one of the slowest regions of the brain to develop. Emotional responses are very much influenced by the amygdala. Through teenage years we learn to regulate our emotions more through developing PFC control and rational thinking. Recent research shows that the PFC does not reach full maturity until our late twenties!

So, before the age of seven, implicit learning is predominant and the brain relies heavily on subconscious processes together with quick assimilation of information though mimicking and repetition. After seven, we increasingly develop our PFC functions and conscious/explicit learning starts to play a key role. We also start to link more to what we know, enabling associative learning and scaffolding.

This is especially relevant in the process of target language acquisition, as according to this associative learning process there should be a constant attempt to associate, wherever possible, target language with native language, and on the contrary to disassociate whenever association leads to something misleading (as in the case of 'false friends', words that sound similar but have different meanings).

From Weber et al.'s previously mentioned 'Alienese' study in 2016, we can conclude that the brain uses the native language as a springboard,

---

[76] Lipton, B, & Bhaerman, S (2010). *Spontaneous revolution: Our positive future and a way to get there from here.* London: Hay House.

in that it relies on familiar grammatical patterns from the native language when processing similar structures in a foreign language. 'We seem to use the same brain areas for native and new language structures.'[77]

So, as language educators, we should be able to:

> constantly stimulate the learning process through provocative association (whenever possible) of native language and target language.

Still in relation to learning, I find it fascinating to consider whether the 'perfect learning state' for the brain actually exists. I personally think it does and that, as educators, we can provoke different learning states in our learners!

Findings on memory formation have been summarised by a model called AGES:[78] Attention, Generation, Emotion and Spacing. The model's creators write: 'With just the right amount of these variables, learners intensively activate their hippocampus, which creates deep circuits for easy retrieval.' This would hint towards a perfect learning state. However, I personally believe that two additional elements should be considered and would strongly recommend adding Intention and Motivation to create the IMAGES model, representing the complete ingredients which are key to maximising learning and moving towards that perfect learning state.

Intention is obviously a necessary ingredient, as without the intention to do something we just would not do it. Additionally, motivation is a critical component of learning. People who are motivated to learn something use higher cognitive processes when learning. These two

---

[77] Weber, K, Christiansen, MK, Petersson, KM, Indefrey, P, & Hagoort, P (2016). fMRI syntactic and lexical repetition effects reveal the initial stages of learning a new language. *Journal of Neuroscience, 36*(26), 6872–6880.

[78] Davachi, L, Kiefer, T, Rock, D, & Rock, L (2010). Learning that lasts through AGES. *Neuroleadership Journal, 3,* 53– 63.

elements can be seen as interconnected, because I may have the intention to do something but I may not be motivated to do it. (May I add the personal example of my strong intention to go running every day, but, believe me, with no motivation to do so?) Conversely, I may have the motivation to do something, but not intend to do it!

> So, IMAGES means:
>
> ➤ enough Intention, Motivation, Attention, Generation, Emotions and Spacing may form the components comprising a 'perfect learning state'.

Together with this concept, I do believe there is also a need to reflect on the ideal brainwaves which should be predominant during this so-called 'perfect learning state'. When masses of neurons communicate with each other, synchronised electrical pulses are generated, producing brainwaves. According to what we are doing or feeling, our brainwaves change. As I mentioned previously, brainwaves can be monitored by an EEG, which measures frequency in hertz.

Here is a simplified overview to explain the different brainwaves:[79]

> ➤ Delta waves are dominant when we are in deepest meditation or dreamless sleep.
>
> ➤ Theta waves also occur during sleep and in deep meditation, and this state is where the gateway to our subconscious lies, thus the gateway to learning and memory.
>
> ➤ Alpha brainwaves are predominant when we go into a quiet, calm consciousness state. If we just take a moment to focus on our breathing, the brain will begin to shift into alpha brainwaves. Alpha indicates a very calm resting state for the brain. In 2015, I had the pleasure of meeting Dr James Hardt, one of the world's

---

[79] There are other brainwaves, in particular gamma brainwaves, but I do not talk about these here. Even though I believe gamma waves are a subject of extreme interest, they are probably better discussed in another book!

leading specialists in brainwaves and biofeedback.[80] Dr Hardt commented to me that 'when the brain is in alpha, it is almost as if the alpha brainwaves massage the limbic system'. From his comment, I understand that if the brain is in alpha, then the limbic system cannot become aroused. Research shows that alpha indicates states of calm and relaxation.[81]

> Beta brainwaves predominate when we are paying attention, making decisions or involved in focused mental activity. Beta brainwaves are divided into three bands: low beta, when we are pondering something; mid beta, when we are actively thinking about something; and high beta, when we are really undergoing complex thought or experiencing high anxiety or excitement. Obviously, when we are about to sit an exam, we can expect to be experiencing mid and high beta brainwaves. Too much beta activity, and especially too much over prolonged periods of time, is negative, leading to stress, anxiety, muscle tension and even insomnia and addiction.

If we speculate for a moment, we could actually think about connecting our potentially perfect learning state with the perfect brainwave activity, to give us the ideal scenario for learning effectively and efficiently. This means the brain would be dancing from predominance of mid beta to low beta to alpha brainwaves. Mid beta would occur when we are working something out, with highly engaging brain activity, then low beta would manifest when we are pondering or musing on the information, and then alpha would indicate the more reflective integration of the learning.

---

[80] More information on Dr James V Hardt can be found on the Biocybernaut Institute's website: www.biocybernaut.com/partners

[81] Kora, P, Meenakshi, K, Swaraja, K, Rajani, A, & Raju, MS (2021). EEG based interpretation of human brain activity during yoga and meditation using machine learning: A systematic review. *Complementary Therapies in Clinical Practice 43*, 101329,ISSN 1744-3881. doi.org/10.1016/j.ctcp.2021.101329.

In fact, research from MIT[82] shows that implicit learning tends to involve theta and alpha waves and explicit learning is more likely to have a predominance of beta brainwaves.

All in all, I would suggest that as neuroeducators we should:

➤ aim for a learner to be in a continuous state of calm and tranquillity together with positive emotions, and thus help the learner into a 'perfect learning state'!

We also need to reflect upon the continuous interplay in our minds between the conscious and the subconscious brain. In his book *The Inner Game of Tennis*,[83] Timothy Gallwey writes about what he calls the thinking brain and the performing brain, and how the thinking brain often interferes with and hinders the performing brain. In terms of language learning, we know that constant attempts in our mind to translate from our native tongue can affect acquisition and fluency of a target language, and when we are able to quieten that 'translating voice' (which also slows us down!), the performing brain may take over and fluency may flourish.

For this reason, I would also suggest that it is always necessary for the neuroeducator to:

➤ get the learner into a state where the subconscious mind is the main performer and the conscious mind takes a back seat.

So, reflecting on all I have mentioned regarding the different aspects of neuroscience, are we in a new era of metacognition and more self-awareness?

---

[82] Loonis, RF, Brincat, SL, Antzoulatos, EG, & Miller, EK (2017). A meta-analysis suggests different neural correlates for implicit and explicit learning. *Neuron 96*(2), 521–534.e7

[83] Gallwey, WT (1997). *The inner game of tennis: The classic guide to the mental side of peak performance*. New York: Random House.

I truly believe that the answer is YES. We are gaining more insights into how our brains react and function and how we learn and, yes, there appears to be momentum for emotional intelligence or social and emotional learning (SEL) and principles of neuroscience to penetrate the learning process. I strongly believe that we are now in a new educational era: one in which the learner no longer has to adapt to the teacher, but the teacher is adapting to the learner(s).

Thirty-five years ago, the field of neuroeducation started to create whispers in the academic world, concretely in 1988 by the formation of the Psychophysiology and Education Special Interest Group. It is now the cornerstone of many research organisations around the world, and educational neuroscience, or neuroeducation, has not only emerged from the whispers but is now fully underway in practice, as evidenced by various people who are marrying neuroscience with education of some type or other.[84]

According to Aalok Mehta, neuroeducation 'is an interdisciplinary field that combines neuroscience, psychology and education to create improved teaching methods and curricula and is moving increasingly close to prime time, as researchers gain a more sophisticated understanding of how young minds develop and learn.'[85]

Focusing in on neuroeducation, the more we are discovering about how the brain works, the more we are able to bring this comprehension into educational methods and approaches, to create brain- friendly conversations and ultimately brain-friendly learning. And that is exactly the philosophy upon which I created the concept of Neurolanguage Coaching.

Based on the knowledge we now have regarding the brain and how the brain likes to learn, we are blasting away those 'neuromyths'[86] that have

---

[84] Mehta, A (2009). Neuroeducation emerges as insights into brain development, learning abilities grow. Published online by the Dana Foundation, NY, USA.

[85] Ibid.

[86] della Chiesa, B, et al. (eds.) (2007). *Understanding the brain: Towards a new learning science*. Paris: OECD.

hindered and disempowered for far too long, and we are now tapping into and encouraging more and more learning potential.

Pettito and Dunbar stated that educational neuroscience 'provides the most relevant level of analysis for resolving today's core problems in education.'[87]

I am sorry that it has taken us 20 years since this research to really start to implement it. And we still have a long way to go before worldwide implementation!

At this point, I would like to suggest that the key is actually in the 'neuroeducators' themselves. I truly believe that once we teachers, trainers and coaches are able to fully understand and embrace the findings with which modern neuroscience and neuropsychology are enlightening us – and fully implement this daily with all of our learners – we will fulfil the parameters for brain-friendly education. In this respect, educators will be much more aware of the impact that we have on our learners.

Over the last year, I have worked with language teachers all over the world, training and certifying them to become Neurolanguage coaches. I have seen teachers absolutely transform with their newly acquired knowledge of the brain and learning. I have witnessed how they really help empower the learner to learn and come into their own full potential. In our case of language learning, this knowledge, together with the incorporation of a coaching style, coaching principles and competencies, notably enhances and potentially utterly transforms the language learning process.

Neurolanguage coaches are bridging the education–neuroscience gap by bringing neuroscience alive in a practical sense and not only in theory. In the 2014 study by Dimitris Zeppos titled 'Profiling Neurolanguage Coaches Worldwide',[88] one of the major findings was

---

[87] Petitto, LA, & Dunbar, K (2004). New findings from educational neuroscience on bilingual brains, scientific brains, and the educated mind. In Fischer, K, and Katzir, T (eds.) (2004). *Building usable knowledge in mind, brain, & education*. Cambridge: Cambridge University Press.

[88] Zeppos, D (2014). Profiling Neurolanguage coaches worldwide – a case study. *World Journal of Education*, 4(6), 26–41.

that most of the people who had been certified as language coaches prior to that study were highly qualified middle-aged teachers, who wanted to bring in change and make a difference to the world. And they truly do!

To summarise the holistic contribution from neuroscientific principles to Neurolanguage Coaching, the Neurolanguage coach fully comprehends and ultimately conveys:

➤ how neurons connect.

➤ how the brain is plastic and can change and develop.

➤ how neurogenesis is possible.

➤ that each learner's brain is unique.

➤ the key roles of the cerebellum, hippocampus and prefrontal cortex in the learning process.

➤ the important role of the amygdala and the absolute significance of the activation of the sympathetic nervous system when in perceived threat situations.

➤ that any type of social or emotional pain or foreign language anxiety in a learner must be accounted for, as this triggered reaction could impact and impede the learning.

➤ how to coach the learner around the perceived threat situation, so that the brain can return to its normal calm and unthreatened state.

➤ how to constantly stimulate the learning process through provocative association (whenever possible) of native language and target language.

➤ that enough IMAGES – Intention, Motivation, Attention, Generation, Emotions and Spacing – may form the components comprising a 'perfect learning state'.

➤ how to aim for the learner's brain to be in a continuous state of calm and tranquillity together with positive emotions and generating the appropriate brainwaves to reflect the perfect learning state.

➤ how to get the learner into a state where the subconscious mind is the main performer and the conscious mind takes a back seat.

The underlying principles of neuroscience pervasive in Neurolanguage Coaching

Drawing upon what I have just highlighted about the brain and how the brain learns, Neurolanguage Coaching is about consciously implementing the underlying principles that will potentially enable an optimal brain state for learning.

Here are the **seven core principles** that are pervasive throughout Neurolanguage Coaching engagements.

1. Striving for the constantly calm brain state

As I have already mentioned, when our brain perceives a threat, whether real or only perceived as real by the brain, the amygdala signals the activation of the sympathetic nervous system. This results in the 'fight-or-flight' response, preparing the body to deal with the threat. In language learning, triggers such as embarrassment, shame or frustration can activate this response. The stress arising from these feelings can hinder cognitive functions like memory, focus and fluency, making language acquisition more challenging.

One such example of a blocked and stressed learner was Juan Miguel,[89] who suffered extreme embarrassment relating to a strong mother tongue accent. He needed English for his profession; in fact, it was a survival question, as without good English he could have lost his job! This affected Juan severely, and he experienced tremendous social pain at work when native English speakers commented on or made fun of his accent. It triggered an overwhelming emotional response in him.

---

[89] Names have been changed to protect the identity of clients.

Juan and I worked together for two years to reduce native accent interference, as well as to build up his confidence and his ability to defend himself, in particular with native English speakers who could not speak any second language (sadly it is normally those people who do not speak another language who criticise the most!). He and I often discussed how the brain was reacting and the emotional triggers involved. We explored how he could deal with triggering situations and build in defence strategies and language tactics. He made excellent progress and shifted from striving to thriving.

Another example can be given from my own language learning experience. I can only describe the scenario as absolute terror to speak in Spanish. When I was 17, I moved to Spain to live. I had mastered written Spanish the two previous years, but could not speak it. In only six months, though, I transformed my written knowledge into spoken, and in the first few years there I became absolutely fluent with hardly any native accent interference. Most people thought I was Spanish!

When I was 20, I was given the opportunity to work in a small Spanish company. Even though I was confidently fluent by then and sounded native, I suffered extreme fear and panic at the thought of answering the telephone. My colleagues thought it was funny, but I blatantly refused to pick up the phone whenever it rang! It took me six full months of courage to answer that phone. Looking back, I now understand that I was suffering from a threat response, which blocked me from behaving in a rational way and provoked 'telephone terror' in my brain.

This is just one example. As I mentioned before, emotional pain and social pain can essentially trigger limbic reactions,[90] which in turn can have an adverse effect on two major regions of the brain: the prefrontal cortex and the hippocampus, which are areas essential to the learning process. Research demonstrates how this happens with maths

---

[90] Eisenberger, NI (2012). The neural bases of social pain: Evidence for shared representations with physical pain. *Psychosomatic Medicine, 74*(2), 126–135. doi.org/10.1097/PSY.0b013e3182464dd1

anxiety.[91] I would propose that this also occurs to the same degree or to an even greater degree for some language learners.

By the way, just the anticipation of doing mathematics triggers a pain response![92] This anticipatory response can significantly diminish working memory capacity and attention, vital for problem-solving and learning. Can you imagine learners who have to give presentations or participate in meetings or conferences in a second language? Just the anticipation of having to do those things may trigger a pain response, especially if the learner feels unprepared or fears judgement. This response could be even more intense than maths anxiety in some cases, as language use is directly tied to self-expression and identity.

As a Neurolanguage coach, if we sense or perceive that our learner is 'triggered', we would engage in a coaching conversation to bring awareness to this emotional response. Firstly, we would explain the fight-or-flight mechanism, and then we would identify and explore the trigger, before moving to strategies to alleviate and normalise.

There are some scenarios in language learning situations which we can instantly recognise as triggers that may activate that fight-or-flight response. Here are some of them.

Potential trigger: Uncertainty

The thought of learning any language could seem an impossible task. It could be that this thought triggers a threat response, as any language learning is in fact an uncertain process by its nature. It could be seen as 'never-ending', given its lack of exact end point. Even with our native language, we could never honestly say that we utterly and completely know the language or will die knowing all of our native tongue! For

---

[91] Ashcraft, MH, & Krause, JA (2002). Math anxiety: Personal, educational, and cognitive consequences. *Current Directions in Psychological Science, 11*(5), 181–185. doi.org/10.1111/1467-8721.00196

[92] Lyons, IM, & Beilock, SL (2012). When math hurts: Math anxiety predicts pain network activation in anticipation of doing math. *PLOS ONE, 7*(10), e48076. doi.org/10.1371/journal.pone.0048076

this reason, target language learning potentially triggers those feelings of a never-ending process. In other words, an immense feeling of uncertainty.

Calming the trigger

Neurolanguage Coaching endeavours to bring the necessary certainty into the process. From the outset, the process is clearly explained to the learner, and we help the learner to understand that the language will be built up step by step. Essentially, we can say that we are going to be 'chunking the language down'.

We conduct skilled coaching conversations that assist the learner in setting their own goals, which are then worked on over a period of time until they are achieved. Once achieved, coach and coachee move on to a new goal-setting process to find the next 'chunks' to work on for another period of time. The learner feels in control of the process and the coach is the sounding-board partner.

Research shows how organising information into chunks reduces cognitive load, allowing for more efficient processing and recall. Chunking not only improves recall of the chunked information but also enhances the recall of other, non-chunked information held concurrently in working memory.[93] George A Miller in 1956[94] theorised that short-term memory has a limited capacity, typically holding the 'magical number' of seven items (plus or minus two). He proposed that we can overcome this limitation by breaking information into larger, meaningful units or 'chunks', to aid memory retention.

In addition, in Neurolanguage Coaching we expertly break down all grammar areas and then build them up in a block-building process.

---

[93] Thalmann, M, Souza, AS, Oberauer, K (2019). How does chunking help working memory? *Journal of Experimental Psychology: Learning, Memory, and Cognition*, 45(1), 37–55. doi.org/10.1037/xlm0000578

[94] Miller, GA (1956). The magical number seven, plus or minus two: Some limits on our capacity for processing information. *Psychological Review*, 63(2), 81–97. doi.org/10.1037/h0043158

Again, this brings more security and certainty and helps the learner feel in control. At all times, we want to keep the coachee calm and believing that they will learn the language in a systematically built up step-by-step fashion, and we offer the necessary structure for the learner to feel constant achievement of goals. This in turn generates a feeling of success, which activates the necessary motivation and inspiration to continue.

Potential trigger: Traditional teacher–student relationship

Another potential threat is the status trigger that could arise from the traditional teacher–student scenario. Previously, teachers were often seen as the ultimate all-knowing experts with a superior status: the sage on the stage! Coaching hinges on the premise that both coach and coachee are of equal status, working together as partners. Sometimes, though, a learner may feel inferior and inadequate.

Calming the trigger

The coach should constantly be acknowledging and giving positive feedback, so that the learner never feels inferior or intimidated. The flowing coaching conversations should allow the learner to feel safe to interact at any time and to express doubts, fears and questions. The coach could also troubleshoot by asking open questions to discover what could help the learner to feel better, or what needs to happen to help the learner improve. There may even be a coaching conversation around building confidence.

Potential trigger: Coach feels threatened by coachee

A situation may arise where, in a reverse of the above, the learner may feel that the coach is not adequate or not qualified enough to be coaching them, and this could even throw the coach into a threat response.

I remember years ago arriving at my first appointment with a board member of an extremely big energy multinational. This person came down to meet me at the reception and then, in the lift, stood far too close for comfort, towering over me, and proceeded to fire questions at me! I remember I calmly stood my ground. I did not move away and responded in a quiet but firm manner.

When I look back now, I understand that scenario as a potential vetting on behalf of my client. Almost as if he were checking me out to see if I was good enough. I subsequently went on to work with this board member for eight years, so I think I passed the test!

Calming the trigger

If there is a scenario in which the client questions your qualifications and capability as the coach, one tactic is to strongly acknowledge the learner's expertise and position; for example, 'You are the expert and, obviously, you know your specialised topic in your own language. I am here to assist you to convert that knowledge into the target language, so in fact I'm here to be your sounding board to enable you to quickly transfer your expertise.' In other words, recognising their status with a little 'factual' flattery will go a long way!

Potential trigger: Group dynamics

Another potential threat trigger is the dynamic in group learning situations. The coach has to ensure that the group feels integrated, maybe with get-to-know icebreakers to start with and then developing their feeling of working in a team, so that the members of the group do not feel threatened by one another. There will be problems in relating to each other and also potential status problems!

Calming the trigger

This can be achieved by introducing group goals, as well as getting the group to establish their rules of behaviour and modus operandi. At all times, the coach should be empathetic with all group members, while maximising the group team dynamic. Open questions to the group and compromise will be the key for a smooth-running group!

Potential trigger: Independent learners

Sometimes a language coach may find that their learner is in fact an independent and quite solitary learner. Sir Winston Churchill famously said, 'I love to learn, but I do not want to be taught.' I have to confess that I am very much one of these people and I do not respond well to being given orders.

Calming the trigger

When faced with such a learner, the coach must be especially careful not to give orders or commands. More often than not, an independent learner will not appreciate being told what to do. In fact, to some people an order is an absolute turn-off or may even trigger the threat status!

The coach must adopt an extremely non-directive style, moving away from the traditional directive, demonstrative teaching style and adopting very calm coaching conversations that perfectly suit the independent learner. In addition, the coach should encourage and support the learner to do as much as possible alone, and should help the learner to feel that the coach is their sounding board. Really finding out what an independent learner likes or wants to do is also essential in this particular case. Open questions will be key for autonomous learners!

Potential trigger: Forced to learn a language

A very common scenario nowadays is one where employees in a company are forced to learn a new target language, which in most cases is English. I have in fact worked in various companies in Europe where the company lingua franca was changed to English.

In this scenario, the Neurolanguage coach is faced with learners who really do not want to be there and who do not want to learn. This can trigger a lot of social pain feelings, which in turn lead to a non-optimal learning state. Children and teenagers may also be forced to learn. In these scenarios, we have to address the unfairness.

Calming the trigger

In these cases, the coach should have an honest conversation with the learner explaining how intention and motivation are absolutely essential for any learning process, and how without these the learning will not be effective. Actually acknowledging the social pain of the learner in this situation will be a first step to demonstrating empathy and an understanding of how the learner feels, which in turn will help the learner to feel their views are appreciated.

Often in this situation, there are strong feelings of unfairness, and, certainly, when a company forces a language on an employee, it is indeed unfair! 'I am really sorry that you are being forced to do this' or 'I can totally understand that you do not want to learn this language' are examples of showing empathy in these scenarios.

Potential trigger: Xenoglossophobia

We have already touched upon foreign language anxiety or 'xenoglossophobia', which may be triggered by speaking, writing, reading or listening to a foreign language.[95]

Calming the trigger

One of the major missions of the Neurolanguage coach is to recognise any sign of a threat response and subsequent negative limbic response and be able to coach the learner around these. That way, the learner can return to a calm, normalised brain state once again, thus ensuring that

---

[95] MacIntyre, PD, & Gardner, RC (1994). The subtle effects of language anxiety on cognitive processing in the second language. *Language Learning*, 44(2), 283–305.

optimal learning will take place. The brain also needs to experience real and personal situations which are relevant to that individual person to make memories stick,[96] as well as positivity, fun and enjoyment to ensure the flow of positive chemicals, in particular dopamine.[97] Dopamine is a crucial neurotransmitter for reinforcing rewarding behaviours, helping to encode new information.

If the learner is really enjoying the process, as well as maintaining a constant calm brain state, then I would suggest that an optimal learning process can take place.

The brain is a creature of habit and automated programmes, so, to really overcome language anxiety, the question to be asked could be 'How can you normalise speaking this language?' The only way that the brain can perceive the target language as 'normal' is by constant practice, exposure and use.

It could also be beneficial to promote translanguaging by the learner (that is allowing the learner to mix target with native language). This will keep the learner calm and also promote code switching in the brain.[98] It will also allow the brain to get used to switching from one language to the other and normalising this activity. This promotes smoother transitions between languages and reduces the cognitive load.

Potential trigger: Not feeling any progress

Another potential trigger could be the lack of visible progress or even of feeling any improvement. Many of our learners may have been

---

[96] Brown, PC, Roediger, HL, III, & McDaniel, MA (2014). *Make it stick: The science of successful learning*. Cambridge, MA: Belknap Press.

[97] Kempadoo, KA, Mosharov, EV, Choi, SJ, Sulzer, D, & Kandel, ER (2016). Dopamine release from the locus coeruleus to the dorsal hippocampus promotes spatial learning and memory. *Proceedings of the National Academy of Sciences, 113*(48), 14835–14840. doi.org/10.1073/pnas.1616515114

[98] Ali, AD (2024). Translanguaging in multilingual university classrooms: Effects on students' language skills and perceptions. *Bilingual Research Journal, 47*(2), 186–210. doi.org/10.1080/15235882.2024.2336942

learning for many years and experience that heavy feeling of frustration.

Calming the trigger

It important to open a coaching conversation with empathy and compassion: 'I am really sorry that you are not feeling as much progress as you would like to feel.' Then I would ask the learner if we could talk about the language learning plateau: the point in learning a language where it feels like progress has slowed or stopped. Many of us have gone through this, but isn't it curious that no one really talks about it?

Interestingly, when we are learning a language, our brain chunks it in through linguistic chunks.[99] The plateau could happen because learners, having reached a fairly high level, need to constantly reinforce and expand linguistic chunks and abstract representations to move forward. As we process language, we come across more complex patterns that the brain struggles to process efficiently, especially if previous chunks have not yet become fully automated. This difficulty could contribute to the experience of a plateau.

By bringing in a professional coaching structure, in the form of goal setting and scheduled goal reviews, the coach can help learners to break language down into more sizeable chunks, so progress can be monitored better. Then learners can notice and celebrate their successes.

To conclude this part, we could refer again to Stephen Krashen's affective filter hypothesis. Krashen's view is that when the affective filter is 'raised' it impedes language acquisition and that 'affective variables' really do influence how the second language is acquired. Emotional triggers can 'raise' the affective filter and form a 'mental block', preventing the learning. Now we know from the research on social

[99] Christiansen, MH, & Chater, N (2016). The now-or-never bottleneck: A fundamental constraint on language. *Behavioral and Brain Sciences, 39*, e62. doi.org/10.1017/S0140525X1500031X

pain and sympathetic nervous system activation that these 'blocks' are the result of the physiological fight-or-flight response.

> A constantly calm brain state is absolutely essential for learning.

2. Motivation is absolutely crucial

Dr Jeffrey Nevid writes:

> *The term motivation refers to factors that activate, direct, and sustain goal-directed behavior ... Motives are the 'whys' of behavior – the needs or wants that drive behavior and explain what we do. We don't actually observe a motive; rather, we infer that one exists based on the behavior we observe.*[100]

Jeanne Ellis Ormrod, in her book[101] *Essentials of Educational Psychology*, highlights:

> *The following general principles which describe how motivation interrelate behaviour, cognition, and learning.*
>
> *Motivation directs behaviour toward particular goals ...*
>
> *Motivation increases effort and persistence and activities ...*
>
> *Motivation affects cognitive processes ...*
>
> *Motivation determines what consequences are reinforcing and punishing ...*
>
> *Motivation often leads to improved performance ...*
>
> *Intrinsic motivation is more beneficial than extrinsic motivation ...*

As Neurolanguage coaches, we know that motivation is a necessary

---

[100] Nevid, JS (2013). *Psychology: Concepts and applications*, 6th ed. Cengage Learning.
[101] Ormrod, JE (2008). *Essentials of educational psychology: Big ideas to guide effective teaching*, 2nd ed. Boston: Pearson, 384–386.

ingredient for any learning process. If we think back to where coaching really originates, namely the sports coach, we have a very clear image of the coach, who is constantly motivating, animating and inspiring the athlete to achieve their goal. This goal may be the cup, winning the race or even just winning the game, but the motivation to win or to achieve is there.

This is what the Neurolanguage coach imitates, and principally what we strive to find is the intrinsic, inner-self motivating factor or factors that will keep our language learner wanting to learn more and more and more. Obviously, the more progress and success the learner experiences, the more that motivation is going to be fuelled.

So, there needs to be an extremely skilful coaching conversation touching upon what the key motivation is for our learner to learn (see section on motivation in part IV). However, there has to be a clear distinction between reasons and the passion, drive, fuel and vision for learning. One of the teachers doing my course in 2024 used the term 'motivision'. I love this! It totally encapsulates the feeling of 'beyond reason and motivation'.

How do we separate out the reasons and tap into the motivision? I often hear teachers saying, 'I motivate my learners,' and I always think we need to be honest. We can entertain and amuse our learners, but we cannot change their intrinsic feelings. Sometimes, even they cannot find that inner passion.

By asking our learners vision questions, we can in fact help them to connect to deeper desires by activating their Positive Emotional Attractor (PEA) state. Research by Richard Boyatzis and Tony Jack discusses how positive emotional states lead to neurological changes that enhance motivation, engagement and learning. The PEA is linked to brain activity that increases dopamine and oxytocin, both of which are associated with positive emotional states that enhance cognitive functions like creativity, decision-making and social connection.[102]

---

[102] Boyatzis, RE, & Jack, AI (2018). The neuroscience of coaching. *Consulting Psychology Journal: Practice and Research, 70*(1), 11–27. doi.org/10.1037/cpb0000095

When we coach for compassion, asking skilful and powerful questions relating to vision, our learners activate networks and regions of the brain that are associated with big-picture thinking, engagement, motivation, stress regulation and parasympathetic modulation.

Motivision taps into the learner's deeper passions, desires and long-term goals. It connects the learner to something that resonates deeply and goes beyond external rewards. This distinction is crucial for engaging learners beyond the surface level of motivation and instead fostering sustained, intrinsic drive.

When I look back through my own language learning journeys, I can clearly detect differing degrees of motivation and motivision.

Learning French at school was something I enjoyed, but there was absolutely no passion and drive that I remotely connected to. My motivation skyrocketed when I developed a very close friendship with a French lady, and that propelled me into unimagined conversations that school had never provided. I remember thinking at about the age of 15, *Wow, I am having girly conversations in French!*

Spanish was a totally different kettle of fish; I fell in love! I confess that was the driving factor for me to become fluent (also knowing that he would not learn English!). This learning was fuelled by the 'motivision' of being in love, going to live in Spain and actually getting married there!

Strangely, living in Catalonia, I had no real motivation to learn Catalan. However, the launch of Catalan TV in the 1980s provided me with implicit learning as the programmes on that channel were much better than the national television!

Years later I was working and living in Italy, and my motivision was extremely high to be able to connect more with the locals and to expand my business in Italy.

My motivation to learn German was extremely low in the first years that I was living in Germany. I found it difficult to connect to the German language; the language pool in my brain was all Latin-based!

On top, all of my friends and language clients there wanted to speak with me in English all the time! After living there some years, when my Italian was flowing, I went deeper into German and discovered the 'Germanic influence' in English, which helped me to springboard and scaffold much more, and my motivation increased.

So, I personally have experienced the impact of real motivation on my language learning journey.

In conclusion, when the language coaching engagement begins, the coach and the learner should have a very deep conversation regarding the learner's intrinsic motivation. The coach has to be skilled enough in this conversation to push to vision and find the motivation. A learner may say that they are motivated to learn English for work, but the coach would push beyond that with a powerful vision question: 'How would speaking fluent English at work change your life?' This type of question normally provokes the vision of a promotion, a relocation or even more frequent travel. Once this intrinsic motivation has been ascertained, the coach should constantly bring the coachee back to this vision and keep reminding the learner of, and connecting with, the learner's motivation throughout the learning process.

Another essential aspect which will assist in maintaining motivation will be the continual setting of language goals and subsequent and periodic review of these. Goal-setting and review will help the learner to recognise progress and success and thus keep the coachee focused on their ultimate vision and motivation to learn the language.

> Motivision is crucial for optimal learning.

One thing to distinguish here is commitment! If you have a learner who says, 'Yes, I am motivated, but I don't have time,' then you need to separate these into two separate coaching conversations: the first to push from motivation to motivision, the second to talk through time management and commitment. Later I will go into more detail on how to conduct these coaching conversations on motivation.

3. Energy flows where attention goes

'Energy flows where attention goes' is a well-known expression with roots in Hermeticism. Hermetic teachings reflect how the power of the mind, focus and intention shape our internal and external reality. It is also a core idea in Huna, a system of thought inspired by ancient Hawaiian practices, which emphasises how the energy you give to your thoughts, feelings and actions creates and directs outcomes in your life.

Interestingly, this expression also aligns with how the brain functions, as it reflects the brain's inherent ability to focus attention, which then directs mental and neural energy to the areas we concentrate on, in this way shaping our experiences, thoughts and behaviours. The more attention we give to the task at hand, the stronger the neural connections relating to that task.[103] Neuroplasticity refers not only to functional changes but also anatomical.[104]

Conversely, the expression 'use it or lose it' reflects how our brain connections weaken when we do not practise something enough.

The Neurolanguage coach is always fully aware that we need enough attention and focus from the learner at all times to ensure the firing and wiring of those neurons. Metaphorically speaking, I always think we are the musical conductor of their 'brain orchestra'.

Constant signposting is one way to ensure that their attention is going into the direction we want it to go. In other ways, guided teaching as opposed to discovery! Guided instruction helps to manage cognitive load, making learning more efficient, whereas discovery learning can

---

[103] Kaufman, SB, & Gregoire, C (2016). *Wired to create: Unraveling the mysteries of the creative mind.* Perigee.

[104] Draganski, B, Gaser, C, Busch, V, Schuierer, G, Bogdahn, U, & May, A (2004). Neuroplasticity: changes in grey matter induced by training. *Nature, 427*(6972), 311–312. doi.org/10.1038/427311a

overwhelm students' working memory.[105] In his book *Visible Learning*, Hattie reports that guided learning techniques have been found to have a greater impact on student achievement than discovery-based approaches.[106]

Another aspect of attention means that that our learner should be free of distractions: the eternal battle against mobile phones pinging or emails and telephone calls! We should strive to get their attention with active, fun, interesting, inspiring learning activities. Variety and novelty[107] can keep the attention level high, as well as visualisation, interactive discussion, relevant and real topics; topics that connect to and affect the learner personally will also help to ensure attention levels. We should always ask the learner what activities they enjoy to maximise the learning with a positive emotional impact.

Additionally, the coach should be aware if the learner seems to have other things on their mind that could potentially interfere with the learning process. At the start of the session the coach could address these issues by saying that they can see that the coachee has a lot on their mind, then pointing out that the session together will only last for 60 minutes (or whatever the programmed time is for the session) and asking the coachee how they would feel if they could leave those issues aside just for this programmed time, so that full attention can be dedicated to the learning process in order to achieve the maximum optimal learning from that session. If you have a business client, I find they connect more readily when you ask them how you can make the session more cost-effective!

I believe that, as coaches, with our heightened levels of empathy, we become sensitive to when we 'lose' our learner. Some years ago, I had a

---

[105] Sweller, J, Ayres, P, & Kalyuga, S (2011). *Cognitive load theory*. Springer Science & Business Media.

[106] Hattie, J (2009). *Visible learning: A synthesis of over 800 meta-analyses relating to achievement*. Routledge.

[107] Jung, SB, & Shelton, AL (2023). Good news! New is good: Novelty as a key feature of advanced academic programs that create positive learner experiences. *Gifted Child Today*, 46(1), 38–47. doi.org/10.1177/10762175221131067

client whose focus and attention, now and then, drifted into issues that were on his mind; I could literally see and sense this. I say that I could see this because his eyes would glaze over; even when he was responding he had that glazed look, and the response would get slower, almost automated. Whenever I noticed this, I would check in with him and say, 'I am sensing that your mind is drifting, and I would just like to check with you if you would like us to have a quick break. Maybe you need to make a note of whatever has just come up for you. I am conscious that you are extremely busy and have a lot on your mind. Can I check if you would like us to have a mini-pause?' Sometimes he would take up the offer, and other times he would bring himself back, pushing those thoughts away and becoming fully present in the language learning again.

Coaching is about constantly checking in with your client, to see what they need at any given time. Research shows that our brains may solidify the memories of new skills we just practised a few seconds earlier by taking a short rest. The results highlight the critically important role rest may play in learning.[108]

I had another client who one day left me totally speechless. I had been with this client for some years already, but that particular day, in the middle of our session, he took me by surprise by telling me that he was a 'power napper' and he desperately needed to take a power nap! The next minute he had fallen asleep, right there in front of me in his chair!

Well, at first I could not believe it and thought he was joking, then I realised that he really was asleep, and I started thinking, *What should I do? Should I leave? How long will he be out?* So I just got on with some agenda setting and checking my next schedules, and about ten minutes later, he came to. Believe it or not, we then picked up and continued from where we had left off, as if nothing had happened, and he was completely lucid and giving the language his full attention again. This experience always reminds me that coaching means no judgements!

---

[108] Bönstrup, M, Iturrate, I, Thompson, R, Cruciani, G, Censor, N, & Cohen, LG (2019). A rapid form of offline consolidation in skill learning. *Current Biology*, *29*(8), 1346–51.e4

As a coach, accept whatever it takes to retain and ensure your learner's attention. We know attention is crucial and the neural networks that get the most attention will be reinforced.

4. Performing brain should take over

If you have gone through the process of learning a language, you will know that there are various stages from beginner to achieving fluency and mastery. If we compare mastery of the language with driving a car, we can see that the two are in fact comparable. After many years of driving a car, an experienced driver performs the activity from a subconscious programme, and no conscious thought is given to any of the necessary tasks for driving that car unless something makes the driver bring in extra concentration and focused attention, like a snowstorm or a hazard on the road.

In his book back in the 1970s,[109] tennis coach Timothy Gallwey identified the thinking brain and the performing brain. He was intrigued by his tennis coachees overthinking and then underperforming, and he suggested that interference from the inner critic/the thinking brain actually negatively impacts performance.

Achieving fluency in a foreign language is the same. When we are flowing with the language, we give no thought to the language spoken; it simply flows from the subconscious with no need to stop, think and translate. (Previously I mentioned that the cerebellum, located at the back of the brain, is involved in verbal fluency.)

Language learning does pass through the uncomfortable stages of firstly needing to really concentrate and think about new grammar, new vocabulary, sentence structure and how all of this fits together. We may experience some discomfort as we try to translate from our native language into the target language in our minds. Slowly parts of the language start to become automatically programmed in such a way that

---

[109] Gallwey, WT (1974). *The inner game of tennis*. Random House.

we do not need to even think about them anymore; the language just spontaneously comes out.

The more we can get our learners into topics that they are passionate about, or topics that are extremely real and personal to them, the more we help them to forget that they are speaking a new language and the more they will go into the flow state. Csikszentmihalyi,[110] often called the father of flow, identified the characteristics of a flow state as:

> ➤ Complete concentration on the task.

> ➤ Clarity of goals and reward in mind and immediate feedback.

> ➤ Transformation of time (speeding up/slowing down).

> ➤ An intrinsically rewarding experience.

> ➤ Effortlessness and ease.

> ➤ A balance between challenge and skills.

> ➤ Actions and awareness merging, losing self-conscious rumination.

> ➤ A feeling of control over the task.

As Neurolanguage coaches, we try to steer our coachee into the flow state and the 'performing brain' as much as we can. There have been times when I have been with clients who have continuously flowed with 'their' topic for 60 minutes in English. At the end of the session I asked them if they realised they had been speaking solidly for 60 minutes in English, and most of them replied that they honestly had not! This, for me, was pure confirmation that the client had been in the flow state during that hour.[111]

The most important thing to remember when trying to achieve the flow state is that the task and the skills must match. If my learner wants

---

[110] Csikszentmihalyi, M (1990). Flow: *The psychology of optimal experience*. Harper & Row.
[111] Egbert, J (2004). A study of flow theory in the foreign language classroom. *Canadian Modern Language Review*, 60(5), 549–586.

to go into a roleplay to practise a certain scenario, we need to ensure that we brainstorm the vocabulary necessary for the learner to be able to 'perform' and flow in that conversation.

One of the real questions for the coach is how to get our learner, firstly, into a relaxed state of mind, so that the limbic system is calm and happy, and secondly, interested enough to flow with the topic and allow the language to come out.

Obviously, you're going to say to me that, if there are words and aspects of grammar missing, the learner will struggle. Even in these cases, though, if the learner feels safe enough to try synonyms or alternative expressions to express themselves, and if the coach allows this without finishing off sentences, interrupting or trying to interfere in any way with the conversation, then the learner builds the trust to go with the flow.

The whole philosophy behind language coaching is to be predominantly engaged in interactive, brain-friendly conversations. I would even suggest that the ratio of talking time should be 70% coachee and 30% coach. The coach is the sounding board, the motivator, the facilitator, the stimulator or 'provocateur' of language.

If you have ever been to a Zumba class, you will witness how the instructors never ever teach the steps. The beginner walks into the room and just has to 'do it'. I am fascinated every time a new person joins the Zumba class, because I observe each time just how quickly people 'do it'. It is absolutely amazing and confirms the power of mirror neurons and action observation.[112] This research suggests that simultaneous performance of action observation and physical practice appears to be the most effective practice condition, because it provides a combined learning effect, which cannot be obtained by either cognitive intervention or physical practice alone.

I firmly believe from my own experience, and from witnessing others, that learning by doing is one of the most powerful ways of learning. In

---

[112] Kim, TH, Cruz, A, & Ha, JH (2011). Differences in learning facilitatory effect of motor imagery and action observation of golf putting. *Journal of Applied Sciences*, *11*, 151–156.

this respect task-based learning and also experiential learning could be employed to engage the learner in reading and speaking.

> By creating a safe space and calm learning, the coach should help the learner to get into the 'just do it' brain state so that the subconscious programmes of the language take over and stimulate the language to start to flow naturally.

5. Chunk it down

We already mentioned that learning a language can potentially throw a learner into a threat state and a negative limbic reaction. We also talked about the fact that language learning is never-ending, and so the Neurolanguage coach will explain to the learner that the language will be broken down into chunks and then built up in a step-by-step block-building process. The language coaching engagement will consist of a rolling process of setting goals, working towards them, and reviewing progress and success, to then repeat the process with new goals. Linguistic chunking will help the learner to pattern the target language.

As a language expert, the Neurolanguage coach also delivers any grammar topic through chunked- down coaching conversations. It is essential for the coach to expertly know how to create the big picture of any grammar area, and then be able to break it down. I always think that traditional grammar books are brilliant but extremely disjointed. I remember one of my top executive clients about 20 years ago, declaring his frustration at all the tenses in English and begging me to help him create a big picture. We did, and it was brilliant, because we were able to place all the tenses on one continuous timeline from past perfect to future! (You can find this in my *Brain-Friendly Grammar* and *Language Coaching in Action* books.)

Even non-grammar topics can and should follow the same principle of 'chunking it down'. Whatever the task, whatever the project, whatever the topic, always break it down so that the brain remains calm and retains the feeling of being capable of achieving what needs to be achieved.

In fact, in Neurolanguage Coaching we have a three-step breakdown process. The first breakdown happens when we are goal setting in the first session with the client. The second happens when we create their schedule, breaking down their chosen goals. The third happens when we go into each individual session and, through conversations, we break down the grammar or other aspects of language on the session agenda.

> Chunking it down is an essential principle for a Neurolanguage coach to follow.

6. Constant connection to target language

We know that the brain learns through association, and the brain tries to connect new information to existing information or existing networks within the brain. It is almost as if the brain is looking for where to place new information in the existing filing cabinets within our minds.

My own language learning experience has helped me to understand the importance associating languages has, and wherever possible I absolutely encourage and promote this. Having learnt Latin, Greek and French at school, all three languages helped me to come into Spanish at the age of 15 when I taught myself the language with my father's 'teach yourself Spanish' books. Of course, as I mentioned before, I had the best motivation anyone can have for learning a language: I was in love with a Spaniard. My first letters to him were an interesting language mix. There was a definite hotchpotch of Latin and French mixed with my attempts at Spanish, which then, over a period of two years, metamorphosed into excellent written Spanish. My consistent connecting and associating of words and grammar from Latin and French really helped me to come quickly into the Spanish language – and I never had one Spanish lesson in my life!

Living in Spain and with constant exposure to Catalan, my brain naturally scaffolded from my French, Latin and Spanish into Catalan.

Years later, I was to experience the same learning by association and disassociation (false friends!) when I transformed my Latinate language pool of knowledge into Italian. I never had one Italian lesson! I just actively began to learn by myself, assisted by frequent periods of time in Italy and then connecting back to my French, Spanish, Catalan and Latin. It took me approximately six months to become fairly fluent in Italian.

A peculiarity worth highlighting here is that at some point, having lived in Spain for 12 years with such a high degree of integration into Spanish life and the Spanish language, Spanish has, in fact, become almost like my base language when learning or speaking other languages. Even more fascinating is the fact that when I speak Italian or French, people often mistakenly think that I am Spanish, because I have a heavy Spanish accent when speaking other Latin-based languages.

Just to add a funny story: about seven years ago I was driving at Lake Garda, Italy, and I was stopped by the Italian police. I presented the officer with my English passport, my German driving licence and German car documents and spoke with him in Italian. With an extremely puzzled expression he asked me, 'Are you English?'

'Yes,' I replied.

'Then why do you speak Italian with a Spanish accent?'

Having an extremely strong Latin pool, however, somehow hindered me coming into the German language. When I lived in Germany, I was trying, without much success, to improve my German. It seemed to be extremely difficult for my brain. I remember pondering on this and trying to pinpoint the reason it was so difficult, and I realised that I needed to shift away from my Latin pool and to connect back to my mother tongue, English, to associate with the Germanic connections in English. Once I understood this, the connections started to flow and my brain started recognising and patterning. It felt like cracking a code!

For example, I began to understand the subtle letter changes in the two languages, giving clues to the exact same word or a similar word. The

German D is often replaced in English by the TH, or the German T with the English D,[113] such as in:

> ➤ thunder – Donner
> ➤ thumb – Daumen
> ➤ thirst – Durst
> ➤ dream – Träume
> ➤ drop – Tropfen
> ➤ reindeer – Rentier

Sometimes just the simple insight of a letter change can lead the brain instantly into associating vocabulary across languages.

Let me give you another example. A few summers ago, I was refreshing my French with one of my certified language coaches, and she gave me the most amazing insight that I had not seen before. She explained that the circumflex accent in French often reflected a missing S from the word, which once existed in old French.[114] For example:

> ➤ hôpital – hospital
> ➤ forêt – forest
> ➤ côte – coast
> ➤ bête – beast
> ➤ dépôt – depot, originating from the Latin word 'deposit'!

What an amazing insight! I had never realised that before, and suddenly my whole French vocabulary has opened up to give me a direct link from potential words that I don't know or didn't think that I knew; just adding that S may lead me directly to the English translation.

Moving on now to another incredible instant booster for beginners learning a Latin-based language: did you know that, just by asking a learner to think about all the English words that end in '-ion', you may have just given that learner the instant key to hundreds of words in

---

[113] This change is known as the High German consonant shift.
[114] Corresponding Norman French words, which in English then retained the lost consonant.

Spanish, French and Italian, among other languages? For example, 'education', 'religion', 'profession', 'illusion' and 'demonstration' are all easily converted into those same words: maybe with a slightly different spelling and pronunciation, but essentially the same words!

As a Neurolanguage coach, we gently provoke the thought process of connecting and associating in our learner wherever possible. This was one of the foundations of the Michel Thomas Method, where target language is linked to equivalents in the native language, and Thomas highlights Latin influences in English to allow learners to incorporate existing vocabulary into the target language. However, Thomas said that this was an 'effective gimmick to get started, but it is not the method'.[115]

On the other hand, connecting target to native could also lead to false connections and false friends. For example, the word 'embarrassed' in English could lead to an association with 'embarazada' in Spanish, which actually means pregnant – a very embarrassing mix-up to make! Therefore, the coach has to bring disassociations to the attention of the learner.

Perhaps the most remarkable false friend for English learners is incredibly the same word in so many languages, yet not English! This is the word 'simpatico' in Spanish, in French 'sympathique', in German 'sympathisch' and in Italian 'simpatico'. The closest English translation is 'nice' or 'friendly', when referring to a person. Most Spanish, French, German and Italian learners of English make the mistake of automatically associating the word with 'sympathetic' – which obviously in English has a totally different meaning. It is amazing to witness how the brain primarily tries to go to what it knows.

Another beautiful demonstration of how the brain tries to springboard from the native language is one that actually tells me if you have a Latin language brain or a Slav language brain! In English we say it depends *on* something, with the preposition 'on'. The Latins would make the

---

[115] Woodsmall, M, and Woodsmall, W (2008). *The future of learning: The Michel Thomas method: Freeing minds one at a time. Great Falls*, VA: Next Step Press, 148.

mistake of saying it depends *of*, whereas the Slavs would say it depends *from*.

Yet another example of this is the word 'als' in German, which means 'than'. When making comparisons, many Germans would say, 'John is taller as Peter.' This is because their brain has directly gone to 'as' due to the similarity with the word 'als'. Usually, when I ask a learner about this mistake and point out the similarity, they instantly understand the reason for choosing the word 'as' and they start to develop an in-built alarm to move into the correct use with the word 'than'.

Having a language coach who fully understands where these connections work and where they don't work speeds up the learning process. Learners have instant insights or 'aha!' moments, which more often than not they **never ever** forget. It is almost like the brain instantly gets it!

Even if the coach knows the answer, they could even ask the learner, 'Where does that mistake come from?' In this way, the learner can realise the reasons behind making a mistake and can work on building bridges to remember the correct language.

So, the language coach constantly provokes connections, by asking the right questions, leading the brain to that associative process, and really helping the brain to connect. The process is the same for grammar points: how is the grammar the same, how is it different, how would the coachee explain the similarity or difference, etc. It is also interesting to understand when a grammar area does not exist in the learner's native language, in which case the coach can explain to the learner that this area will need to be built up from scratch and may feel hard to grasp.

I am conscious that the practice of association may go against the grain of the more traditional ways of teaching languages where the philosophy is that the mother tongue should not be used. I do agree that as much target language as possible should be used, so I am not proposing the constant use of native. What I am proposing is asking the powerful questions to provoke native/target insights.

In conclusion, in my humble opinion, constantly connecting our learner with both target and native language is essential for the language learning process. As previously mentioned, the 2016 research led by Kirsten Weber in Nijmegen gave insights into how the brain goes to the mother tongue's grammar areas to try and springboard into a new language.[116]

A relatively new concept created around this principle of connecting languages is language bridging: 'guiding students to engage in contrastive analysis of the two languages and transfer the academic content they have learned in one language to the other language.'[117]

We should always ask a learner what other languages they already know, because they may even be able to springboard into the target with other language knowledge. Again, referring to my own language experience, I was intrigued to discover that in fact learning Greek at school has helped me come quickly into the Cyrillic alphabet, and into many Russian words too!

> Constant provocation to connect target language to native can greatly enhance the language learning process.

7. Know thy brain and understand that the brain loves habit!

Personally, the more I know about my own brain, the more I understand myself. As I look back through my life, I can now fully comprehend and explain certain reactions, certain situations and certain behaviours.

---

[116] Weber, K, Christiansen, MK, Petersson, KM, Indefrey, P, & Hagoort, P (2016). fMRI syntactic and lexical repetition effects reveal the initial stages of learning a new language. *Journal of Neuroscience, 36*(26), 6872–6880.

[117] Beeman, K, & Urow, C (2012). A third way – the third space – immersion educators and bridging between languages. University of Minnesota. archive.carla.umn.edu/conferences/past/immersion2012/handouts/UrowBeeman_ThirdWay_Handout_Oct2012.pdf

Perhaps one of the most interesting insights for me is that my brain definitely needs the real and practical to be able to absorb and understand the learning. I can see that I was an excellent learner of theory, but then had great difficulty transforming that theory into practice, and I really needed an extreme personal reason or motivation for my brain to want to come into that practical understanding.

Metacognition, according to Costa, is about 'becoming aware of one's own actions and their effects; posing internal questions to find information and meaning; developing mental maps, pictures, or plans; monitoring plans throughout a process and revising plans when they are not working; self- evaluating a completed plan'.[118] Hattie says that 'we need to develop an awareness of what we are doing, where we are going, and how are we going there; we need to know what to do when we do not know what to do. Such self-regulation, or meta-cognitive skills are one of the ultimate goals of all learning.'[119]

There have been numerous other insights that I have had (as previously stated) regarding my language learning experience, as well as recognising deep subconscious brain patterns that I unwittingly assumed as a child. These patterns had an impact on most of my life until now,[120] when I have been able to recognise and alter them.

Additionally, through the years, I have recognised how I react to fear: how my limbic system used to throw me into panic every time I got on an aeroplane, for example, and how I then discovered how to calm my fear of flying to finally reach the breakthrough of flying with no fear whatsoever. I forced myself to fly every week by taking on work in Italy while living in Germany, and I trained my brain to go into a calm, meditative state every time I got on a plane. After a few times, it became routine for my brain – like getting on a bus or a train! Now,

---

[118] Costa, AL (2008). *The school as a home for the mind: Creating mindful curriculum, instruction, and dialogue.* Thousand Oaks, CA: Corwin Press.

[119] Hattie, J (2012). *Visible learning for teachers: Maximizing impact on learning.* Routledge.

[120] De Bellis, MD, & Zisk, A (2014). The biological effects of childhood trauma. *Child and Adolescent Psychiatric Clinics of North America, 23*(2), 185–222. doi.org/10.1016/j.chc.2014.01.002

I thoroughly enjoy flying, and I am also capable of being so relaxed and so peaceful on a plane that I fall asleep. That must be one of my greatest achievements in life: the battle of overcoming an extreme fear.

The reason I am saying all this is because I have realised that the more I know about my brain, the more effectively I can optimise how I work and how I learn. I have also noticed over the years that the more I share about the knowledge of the brain with my clients, the more fascinated and engaged they become, and in addition they start to understand more about how *they* themselves think and learn. We have to remember that everybody's brain is different. The learner sitting in front of us each time will be absolutely unique and may learn in a totally different way to the next learner with us.

In this way, the Neurolanguage coach shares, whenever relevant, information regarding:

- How the brain makes connections and neuroplasticity.
- How the sympathetic nervous system may be activated.
- How the brain can feel blocked during the learning process.
- How to keep attention high.
- How to connect with the motivision.
- Any relevant information that could really help the learner to know and understand themselves better.

Above all, we need to remember that the brain is, in essence, a creature of habit. In 2003 I made a life decision to move to Germany, to a country which was totally new to me. I could not speak the language and had no idea whatsoever of how my new life would be. One of the greatest, and at the same time simplest, of tips was given to me from an amazing source (one could say divine intervention!): 'Create habits and routines as quickly as possible, and your transition into your new life will be smooth.' I consciously followed that advice and by day three had started to forge my new routines. Sure enough, within one week I was feeling settled and my brain was calm.

Knowing about our own brain and respecting its nature as a 'creature of habit and subconscious programmer' will greatly assist our learner in getting to know their brain.

In summary, these are the seven underlying principles of neuroscience which are constants within the Neurolanguage Coaching process:

➤ A constantly calm brain state is absolutely essential.

➤ Motivision is crucial for optimal learning.

➤ Ensure the learner's attention. We know that this is crucial, because the neural networks that get the most attention will become stronger.

➤ Get the learner into the 'just do it' brain. This means that the subconscious programmes of the language take over and stimulate the language to start to flow naturally.

➤ Chunk it down! Whether it's the process of language learning or the mechanical grammatical breakdown of the language itself, this still applies.

➤ Constant provocation to connect target language to native can greatly enhance the language learning process.

➤ Knowing about our own brain and respecting its nature as a 'creature of habit and subconscious programmer' will greatly assist our learner in getting to know their brain.

Part III

What is coaching?

The etymological origins of the word 'coaching' come from the Hungarian word *kocsi* ('of Kocs').[121] According to historians, the coach was named after the small Hungarian town of Kocs, famous for cart building and transport between Vienna and Budapest. In fact, this meaning is exactly the underlying philosophy of modern-day coaching: that is, to get someone from point A to point B.

In the 1830s the 'coach' referred to an academic tutor,[122] supporting a student with their academic work. Seemingly, in the mid-nineteenth century, William Hopkins became the first private tutor fostering a 'coaching approach' at the University of Cambridge.

By the mid-nineteenth century, the term began to be applied to sports, especially in Britain, where the status of sports was upgraded in that Victorian period. To professionalise sports, a 'coacher' had to become established, and the word 'coach' began to be used in boat races, particularly 'the Boat Race' between the teams of the University of Oxford and the University of Cambridge on the River Thames.

For me, the essential spirit of coaching was born at that point. The coach as the figure to empower and unleash the potential of the coachee, encouraging and supporting them to reach their goals. However, sports coaches can be quite directive and mandatory!

Life coaching as a structured profession started to emerge in the 1970s. One key figure who contributed to this was Werner Erhard,[123] who founded Erhard Sensitivity Training (EST). This was a series of weekend seminars to help participants achieve personal development and transformation, aimed at creating breakthroughs challenging beliefs, emotional blocks and ways of thinking. The empowerment

---

[121] Online Etymology Dictionary. Coach. etymonline.com/index.php?term=coach
[122] Ibid.
[123] Born John Paul Rosenberg.

achieved through EST aligned with the theories of self-actualisation[124] and self- determination,[125] which are central to coaching.

The second key figure in the birth of coaching was tennis coach Timothy Gallwey, who successfully published *The Inner Game of Tennis* in 1974. Through his experience coaching people in tennis, Gallwey realised that if we reduce directives or instructions or even 'transfers' of technical knowledge, learners learn faster and achieve improved performance.

Sir John Whitmore was a British racing driver whose experience in competitive sports influenced his belief in the importance of mindset and performance. He moved into business consultancy and coaching and studied psychology and human potential development. He was fascinated by Gallwey's work and went to see him in Ireland. This meeting had a significant impact on Whitmore's approach to coaching. Gallwey's work inspired Whitmore to develop the first ever coaching model – GROW – in the 1980s. Whitmore became a thought leader in applying coaching techniques to business and leadership and in 1992 wrote one of the first books in coaching, *Coaching for Performance.*[126]

The third key figure in the development of life coaching was Thomas Leonard, often called the 'father of life coaching'. He worked as a financial planner and offered consultancy but noticed that his clients needed support for personal and professional challenges. In this way, he moved beyond financial advice into 'life coaching' and founded the Coach University in 1992.

Leonard later helped to establish the International Coach Federation (ICF) in 1995. This was and is a non-profit organisation with the objective of setting out the standards, ethics and certification processes for the coaching profession. By 1996, there were 60 ICF chapters

---

[124] Maslow, AH (1954). *Motivation and personality.* Harper & Row.

[125] Deci, EL, & Ryan, RM (1985). *Intrinsic motivation and self-determination in human behavior.* Springer.

[126] Whitmore, J (2009). *Coaching for performance: GROWing human potential and purpose,* 4th ed. Nicholas Brealey.

worldwide. In 1997 ICF Credentialing began, and in 1999 ICF accredited coach training programmes.

In 2023, the coaching industry market size was at ~$5.34B with a predicted market size of ~$6.25B in 2024. The ICF's 2023 report estimated $4.65B revenue in 2022 generated by coach practitioners. This represented a 60% increase from the 2019 estimate of $2.85B.[127]

The study also estimated approximately 126,050 active coaches in 2023 and predicted approximately 145,500 active coaches in 2024.[128]

One thing to mention is that coaching is not a regulated profession, so actually anyone can call themselves a coach. For this reason, institutions such as the ICF, through their credentialing and accredited programmes, set the standards for professional training in this field. Other established coaching bodies are the International Authority for Professional Coaching & Mentoring (IAPC&M), the Center for Credentialing & Education (CCE), the European Mentoring & Coaching Council (EMCC), the International Association of Coaching (IAC) and the Association for Coaching.

There are many definitions of coaching. For example, the ICF definition:[129]

Partnering with clients in a thought-provoking and creative process that inspires them to maximize their personal and professional potential. The process of coaching often unlocks previously untapped sources of imagination, productivity and leadership.

Another from Sir John Whitmore:

Coaching means unlocking a person's potential to maximise their own performance; it is helping to learn rather than teaching them.

---

[127] ICF's 2023 Global Coaching Study, ICF's 2020 Global Coaching Study, IBIS World's Business Coaching Industry in the US Report, IBIS World's Life Coaches Industry in the US Report.

[128] Ibid.

[129] International Coaching Federation (2025). Read about ICF. coachingfederation.org/about ICF Competencies 2021

The ICF also has a vision statement, 'A world where coaching is integral to transforming societies,' and a mission statement: 'We advance coaching excellence, impact, and value worldwide.'

In 1998 the ICF Core Competencies were identified by eight pioneers in the coaching industry to provide a standardised foundation and framework for professional coaching. In 2008, a job analysis was conducted by the ICF but no changes were introduced to the competencies. However, in 2019, there was another job analysis with more than 1,300 coaches across the globe, ICF members and non-members. The empirical data collected validated the original ICF Core Competency model but also reflected current coaching practices and resulted in a new competency model. This new model was implemented from 2021.

ICF Competencies 2021

A. Foundation
    1. Demonstrates Ethical Practice
    2. Embodies a Coaching Mindset
B. Co-Creating the Relationship
    3. Establishes and Maintains Agreements
    4. Cultivates Trust and Safety
    5. Maintains Presence
C. Communicating Effectively
    6. Listens Actively
    7. Evokes Awareness
D. Cultivating Learning and Growth
    8. Facilitates Client Growth

Nowadays, it really can be said that the coaching profession and industry is continually growing and spreading into a vast array of disciplines. Coaching is extensively used in the corporate world, where leadership coaching, executive coaching, business coaching and team coaching are commonly pursued. Additionally, over recent years we have heard a lot of new types of coaching, for example health coaching, spiritual coaching, career coaching, systemic coaching, relationship coaching, interview coaching – the list is endless, and coaching appears to be invading all walks of life.

At this point, I would also like to clarify what coaching is not. Coaching is not therapy, counselling or psychotherapy of any kind, nor is it consulting or training or mentoring. It is not about giving advice or telling someone what to do! The coach is the soundboard. The facilitator. The provocateur of insights and 'aha!' moments. The non-judgemental accompanying partner assisting the coachee in finding their own solutions, setting their own goals and revealing their own journey towards achieving these.

Therapy and counselling mostly analyse the past, focus on an event or aspect of a person's past and work on comprehending, healing, resolving, improving or recovering. The professionals in these fields offer guidance, give advice or provide a course of action.

In contrast, coaching deals with the whole person's performance and aspirations, whether personal or professional, and is primarily present and future-oriented. Fundamentally, coaching deals with the 'now' and the immediate future. A coach will 'fact-find' to ascertain the current situation, maybe to gain insight into how past events may have influenced the present, but then will mostly push to vision and solutions to promote client growth and transformation.

These are some of the principles of being a great coach:

- ➤ Excellent active listener.
- ➤ Empathetic at all times.
- ➤ Expert at posing the right questions at the right moment.
- ➤ Capable of creating mood, climate and safe setting for coachee.
- ➤ Sees the coachee as equal.
- ➤ Engages the coachee to be motivated.
- ➤ Is a flexible resource for the coachee.

- Allows the coachee to feel in control of their process.

- Provokes ongoing thoughts.

- Responds with emotion and empathy.

- Able to deliver continual positive feedback and acknowledgement.

- Holds absolutely no judgements.

- Sustains great use of coaching conversations.

- Recognises their own limitations.

- Honest at all times.

What about coaching in education? Business and life coaching possibly began to influence coaching in education in the 1990s. It became more structured and evidence-based, drawing from fields like positive psychology and emotional intelligence. It was used to improve student performance and motivation as well as to support teacher professional development.

Jim Knight defines educational coaching as 'a collaborative partnership between coaches and educators to improve instructional practices and student learning outcomes'.[130] Elena Aguilar describes coaching as 'a tool for supporting educators in achieving transformation through reflection, collaboration, and goal-setting'.[131] Educational coaches were often introduced as an agent of change and through the years, as teachers have integrated more coaching practices, there has been less 'sage on the stage' teaching as 'the most effective teachers create opportunities for learning by allowing students to discover knowledge in a mutually supportive environment'.[132]

---

[130] Knight, J (2007). *Instructional coaching: A partnership approach to improving instruction.* Corwin Press.

[131] Aguilar, E (2013). *The art of coaching: Effective strategies for school transformation.* Jossey-Bass.

[132] Ellis, EL, & Smith, KL (eds) (2020). *Coaching copyright.* American Library Association.

Over the past 30 years, the more common approach in instructional and educational coaching has involved a coach working with teachers to support their professional growth and improve instructional practices. Often these coaches have been former teachers or administrators with significant classroom experience. The coaching centres upon enhancing teaching strategies, classroom management and student outcomes.[133] Multiple benefits have resulted from this type of coaching. For example, personalised support tailored to the teacher's needs, or reflective practice and improved teaching effectiveness.

Nowadays, I would suggest that there is a growing trend for teachers themselves to undergo coach training to transform their teaching into a coaching approach. This is exactly the case for Neurolanguage coaches. Personally, I think we are collectively shifting education into a new era. We are moving away from the time that learners had to adapt and adjust to the teacher. Now, we, the educators, are adapting to our learners! I would suggest this is very different to the educational coaching of the past 30 years whereby the teacher received coaching and then implemented 'insights gained' from those coaching sessions. I would even go so far as to say that a new educator persona is emerging: 'the coacher'.

The coacher receives professional coach training and transforms the learning process through:

> Changing the structure of the learning by incorporating goal settings, activity settings and goal reviews.

> Embracing the spirit of coaching with conversation that promotes a growth mindset, empowering and unleashing learning potential.

> Promoting learner autonomy and self-regulated learning processes.

> Addressing motivation and commitment.

---

[133] Costa, AL, & Garmston, RJ (1994). *Cognitive coaching: A foundation for renaissance schools*. Christopher-Gordon.

> ➤ Being a neutral, non-judgemental soundboard and accountability partner.

> ➤ Harnessing critical thinking through Socratic questioning and provoking insights.

Language coaching and Neurolanguage Coaching

We can definitely see the development of the phenomenon of language coaching in today's language market.

Neurolanguage Coaching was born in the year 2012 with the pilot course in Düsseldorf with my team of 12 language teachers. In 2013, the first groups of teachers took the course in Paris, London and online. Right from the beginning, this course was launched with accreditation from the International Coach Federation and was therefore one of the first ever language coaching courses to carry an accreditation from a recognised coaching body.

However, Neurolanguage Coaching not only integrates professional coaching into its process, but also integrates and implements neuroscientific research, neuropsychology and emotional intelligence, with the result that both coaching and neuroscience are woven into the language learning process. This means that this particular approach goes beyond just using coaching competencies, principles, models and techniques. It also has no grey area confusing language coaching with life coaching, as the full focus is to learn, enhance and improve a language.

So, what are the differences between coaching, language coaching and Neurolanguage Coaching?

Coaching, whether life or business coaching, centres upon personal questions, issues, dilemmas and/or goals. Language coaching implies that a target language is being learnt, improved or developed, and there must be a definite focus on coaching around a 'language'.

So, in theory, what is language coaching? As a generic term, there may be various definitions, but it could be said that language coaching transports elements and principles from the coaching field and integrates them into the language learning process. Such elements and principles may be coaching models or the structure of a coaching engagement, which would involve goal-setting processes and action-setting processes together with a setting of time periods' and a clear management of coaching engagements. The coach may or may not possess coaching training and may actually be an expert language teacher calling themselves a coach.

I sometimes hear confusion between life coaching and language coaching, and for this reason I do think it is essential to be clear on the definitions of both. The confusion is fuelled by language trainers conducting 'life coaching' sessions in a target language and calling this language coaching. I beg to differ. This is life coaching in a target language. The critical point in these sessions is 'where is the focus of my coachee's brain?' Is it on the life coaching dilemma or is it on the language improvement?

In such a case, there should be a clear delineation of the purpose of the coaching contract and the focus of the ensuing sessions, so that the expectations of the client may be met. In addition, there is definitely a difference in pricing, as life coaching may command extremely high fees!

How is language coaching different to Neurolanguage Coaching?

Neurolanguage Coaching goes beyond language coaching. On the one hand, it incorporates all the elements, principles, models, ICF standards, ICF competencies and ethics. On the other hand, it integrates findings and principles of neuroscience and neuropsychology as well as emotional intelligence into the language learning process. Brain-friendly coaching conversations are adopted throughout, even when transferring knowledge from the coach to the coachee.

In 2012, I created the definition of Neurolanguage Coaching as 'the efficient and fast transfer of language knowledge with sustainable effects from the language coach to the language coachee, facilitated by brain-based coaching and coaching principles as vehicles'.

In summary, it can be said that Neurolanguage Coaching:

> - Harnesses all aspects of professional coaching to create a safe and trustworthy learning space for language learners.

> - Integrates the ICF competencies, guidelines and ethics into the process.

> - Has a unique structure that centres upon a first session with the client and thereafter partnering with the learner to achieve their goals.

> - Promotes learner autonomy and self regulated learning.

> - Weaves neuroscience and neuropsychology into the process.

> - Uses coaching conversations wherever necessary to troubleshoot.

What Neurolanguage Coaching is not!

At this point it could be interesting (and necessary) to clarify that Neurolanguage Coaching is not:

1. Just working through a language book

In general, Neurolanguage Coaching is really about the coach being the resource. The whole engagement should consist of continuous coaching conversations in which there is an interplay between the mechanical side of the language (grammar) and the mastery side of the language (application). Of course, materials can be introduced; however, these should only be used as provocations to trigger the coaching conversations and not used as the main or only focus of a session. The ideal scenario would be for the coach and coachee to create their own materials together. 'The one who does the work does the learning.'[134]

2. A traditional teacher/student relationship

Across the globe, there is a definite shift away from the traditional teacher–student relationship. In the past, however, there was a certain 'superiority' of the teacher, with a more passive role of the learner. This drastically changes in the coach–coachee relationship, which is a relationship of equal status.

In a session, there should ideally be at least 70% spoken participation from the learner in relation to a 30% input from the coach. This ensures that the learner is incredibly active throughout a Neurolanguage Coaching engagement.

---

[134] Doyle, T (2011). *Learner-centered teaching: Putting the research on learning into practice.* Stylus.

I have had countless clients who have complained to me about previous trainers who spent most of their session talking about themselves and hogging the conversation. This totally defeats the object of language learning and can also put the learner off speaking.

3. A life-coaching session

We already mentioned that Neurolanguage Coaching is *not* a life-coaching session. There has to be focus and connection to language learning, whether on the grammatical side of the language or the application of the target language. For instance, a coachee may have an extremely high level of English but need to improve delivering presentations. The coach could go beyond the subject of English and also include questions regarding delivery, style or overcoming nerves, but the focal point would still be enhancing the final presentation in the target language.

In my own experience, I have indeed had clients who come to the language coaching session and want to discuss their personal problems. I know this happens daily to thousands of language trainers, teachers or coaches, and many of the people who have taken my course share this experience.

In this particular case, it is necessary for the language coach to bring the focus and attention of the coachee back to the language learning. This can be done quite subtly by asking the coachee whether they would like to continue with that personal conversation, but whether you, as the coach, could analyse the language. So, you would take note of any mistakes and, every now and then, ask the coachee to give their own feedback and then ask permission to share your observations and the mistakes you had noticed. In this way, the coach gently but firmly brings the focal point back into the mission of language learning.

Alternatively, the coach may highlight their concern about cost-effectiveness in relation to improving the language and gently persuade the coachee to come back into a language focus by introducing the goals that have been previously agreed by the coachee.

4. A psychological process like therapy or mentoring

As mentioned above, Neurolanguage Coaching has nothing to do with therapy or mentoring.

Interestingly, when I first started to develop the concept of language coaching and Neurolanguage Coaching in Germany in the mid-2000s, new concepts were frowned upon by certain HR employees and purchasing department employees. It was considered absolutely taboo to put coaching together with language because, in Germany, coaching was considered to be an extremely confidential process which no one should talk about. In addition, only professional coaches who had a higher university degree or diploma were 'accepted'.

So, when I began to introduce language coaching, following the ICF concept of coaching, some Germans did not like it, nor did they accept it. I later understood that the same phenomenon also existed in other countries, for example France.

In one meeting (which actually lasted two hours) with a purchase manager in Germany in 2011, I was attacked, insulted, humiliated and shot down for connecting coaching to language. My secretary at that time was with me in the meeting, and afterwards we both sat in my car, looked at each other and burst into tears!

Nevertheless, this meeting was key: it brought out my sheer determination to prove that language coaching existed. It served as the motivational driver for me to clearly crystallise, delineate and define this new concept of language coaching, and then to further enhance it with the principles of neuroscience to differentiate Neurolanguage Coaching from ordinary language coaching.

5. A consultancy session

There are many extremely qualified professionals who are now turning to the fields of language coaching and Neurolanguage Coaching. Some are lawyers and specialise in the field of legal language coaching. Others are ex-professionals from the finance industry, accountants, investment bankers etc., and all of these ex-professionals are bringing their professional expertise into a specialised language coaching arena.

These particular individuals will always have to ensure that language coaching engagements remain as such, and that they do not wander into any type of consultancy at any time. Consultancy would probably require professional indemnity insurance and, in addition, consultancy would command significantly higher fees.

6. Just a chat!

Neurolanguage Coaching is not just having a conversational chat with clients. It may be that our learners do want to focus on the spoken aspects of language much more than the written or grammatical parts of language. However, the coach must always ensure that any conversation has a definite focus as well as a definite structure. In addition, the conversation must have intervals where the coach/coachee interaction comes into feedback and analysis of the language that was used, the difficulties faced, the positive aspects of the language used and any other observations that can help the learner to comprehend and correct their language knowledge and use.

The bottom line is that all conversation must have an underlying purpose and direction that is clearly voiced and steered by the coachee. This keeps the brain focused on a clear purpose and desired outcome for that conversation.

The differences between language teaching and Neurolanguage Coaching

Neurolanguage Coaching aims to enhance language teaching or training. However, it must never be forgotten that there is a theoretical and grammatical part of language learning in which the Neurolanguage coach will have to explain grammatical principles and constructions, and the coach will often need to touch upon a necessary teaching element of language learning.

In some ways, teaching and coaching are at opposite poles, as 'coaching is non-directive, where the answer is not known and waiting to be discovered, while teaching is directive, with an idea of the path learners are on and the questions that will be asked'.[135]

The difference in Neurolanguage Coaching comes from:

> ➤ How the material is delivered.

> ➤ How the Neurolanguage coach captures and directs the attention of the coachee.

> ➤ How the Neurolanguage coach facilitates brain connections through provoking associations.

> ➤ How the Neurolanguage coach builds rapport and dialogues with the coachee so that the brain is never triggered into a threat status response.

In 2014 Dimitris Zeppos wrote an article about the profile of Neurolanguage coaches[136] and created a table demonstrating the

---

[135] Ellis, EL, & Smith, KL (eds) (2020). *Coaching copyright*. American Library Association
[136] Zeppos, D (2014). Profiling Neurolanguage coaches worldwide – a case study. *World Journal of Education*, 4(6), 26–41.

principal differences between language teaching and language coaching. In the left-hand column we can see the characteristics of Neurolanguage Coaching in contrast to those of traditional-style teaching.

Table 1: Comparison between Characteristics of Neurolanguage Coaching and Traditional Language Teaching

Language coaching	Language teaching
• Active learning • Motivation takes top priority • Empathy	• Passive
• Coach has ability to keep client engaged, motivated, valued and committed	• It could sometimes be described as a mainly one-way process
• Client takes responsibility and ownership • Flexible and self-directed	• Book related – following chapters and the order of language learning books
• Normally no books are used	• Often limited to materials/books used
• There is an equal status of coach and learner • There is an awareness of limitations • Matches the needs of the client	• Teacher takes the role of the expert, denoting a superior status • The relationship between teacher and the learner is often not so close, nor is it a realistic or personalised experience • Often encompasses a more formal approach
• 'Teaching' is kept to a minimum • Continuous feedback and acknowledgement • Stimulates reflexion	• Instructive and mandatory • Directional • Demonstrative

• Coach has the ability to adapt to the client • Client focused and tailor-made	• With groups – often trial and error – not tailored to individuals • Often the subject must be learnt, so the teacher is interested in the topic but the learner is not
• One objective is to maximise the potential of the learner	• Often does not take into account the social context and cultural interaction of the learner
• Focus on cost-effectiveness	• Normally not cost-effective and no awareness relating to cost-effectiveness

Over these past 12 years working with teachers across the globe, I have witnessed more and more how language teachers are naturally and intuitively shifting into a coaching approach without realising it. Personally, I think it is to adapt to the learners of today, as the traditional methods are no longer effective.

Upon completing my course to become a Neurolanguage coach, these intuitive teachers are then able to realise what they were doing and how to become conscious of it and enhance it to produce even more impact on the learning.

In essence, teachers who gain knowledge of traditional coaching and brain-friendly coaching conversations and then transform into Neurolanguage coaches become:

> ➤ Aware of how the brain learns.

> ➤ Aware of their own impact as an educator on the learner's brain.

> ➤ Sensitive to 'limbic threat reactions' of the brain.

> ➤ Provocative, provoking brain connections.

> ➤ Experts at powerful brain-friendly conversations.

> ➤ Experts at active listening, in particular active listening on

various different levels, bearing in mind that the Neurolanguage coach is listening to content as well as linguistic abilities, mistakes, grammar and sentence constructions.

> Not only empathetic but also able to go into compassionate coaching conversations.

> Aware of coaching competencies, ethics and principles.

> Masters in goal-setting conversations.

> The soundboard, no longer telling their coachees what to do.

> Non-directive, less demonstrative and much more interactive and passive (as the learner takes the role as the active participant).

> The catalyst and facilitator of the learning.

> Structured and orientated towards focus and attention, always artfully steering the brain into a focused 'reason' for all conversations.

Part IV

The process and structure of Neurolanguage Coaching

The theoretical spiral learning process

The process of a Neurolanguage Coaching engagement moves forward in cycles. This is reflected in the PROGRESS[137] model, which clearly explains the progressive spiral learning process. The model can be used to reflect the process to the learner so that they can fully appreciate this.

PROGRESS stands for:

P – Practise

R – Repeat

O – Ongoing

G – Goals

R – Remember

E – Emotions

S – Success

S – Start again

Broadly speaking, the process involves initiating from a two-tier goal-setting process, which focuses on the mechanical and mastery aspects of the language. The goals are set by the coachee, although the coach expertly conducts the goal setting. The coachee also indicates a realistic time period in which to achieve those goals. The coach then creates the personalised roadmap and plan for the learner and, following these, the learning process commences.

---

[137] © Rachel Marie Paling 2012.

The goals are worked on during the given time period and, once this period comes to an end, a goal review is held to check on the coachee's progress. If the coachee feels that the goals have been reached, then new goals are set and the whole process recommences. The spiral process from goal- setting to goal-setting involves chunking down the language into bite-size goals, which, as we know, keeps the limbic regions calm and the brain able to focus better.

The coachee **Practises** and **Repeats** the **Ongoing Goals** that are continually being set. Through this practice and repetition, the coachee **Remembers**, and positive **Emotions** ensure the right chemical processes in the brain to assist the long-term memorisation. Achieving the goal signifies **Success**, and a new topic is introduced and the process **Starts again**. The intention is that every cycle takes the coachee deeper into the language, constantly improving and advancing. One of the most important factors is that the coachee is able to subjectively measure and feel the success of the goals, as this inspires and motivates the coachee to learn more.

The imagery behind this process is the movement of a progressive forward-moving spiral. The learner will never come back to the same point once the goals have been achieved; they will always come to a point further down the line. If the goals have not been achieved then the movement forward is less, but nevertheless there is always some progress. Learner autonomy is key throughout!

The essential conversations of Neurolanguage Coaching

Neurolanguage Coaching comprises three essential conversations: Motivation, Mechanics and Mastery, which I have labelled the 3Ms or the 3 MUSTS.

When working with a learner or group of learners, the first session is absolutely crucial! In this first session, we firstly create a safe and trustworthy space and then we go into a skilled conversation around motivation to reveal the learner's motivision. After this, we transition into two goal-settings, the first a focused mechanical goal-setting (grammar areas) and the second an extremely well-steered mastery goal-setting (functional language).

Motivation

We have already noted that motivation is essential for the learning process.[138] It is crucial for multiple reasons. It kickstarts the learning, as it arouses curiosity and interest in the language, and it also increases engagement. From the physiological perspective it promotes the production of dopamine, and this is essential for memory formation and retention. It harnesses persistence, as a clear vision will help fuel the learning even through difficult moments. It fosters self-directed learning and learner autonomy[139] and connects the learning to real and personal goals.

For this reason, the coach, at the beginning of the coaching engagement, must have a deep and powerful conversation with the

---

[138] Pintrich, PR, & De Groot, EV (1990). Motivational and self-regulated learning components of classroom academic performance. *Journal of Educational Psychology*, *82*(1), 33–40. doi.org/10.1037/0022-0663.82.1.33

[139] Deci, EL, & Ryan, RM (1985). *Intrinsic motivation and self-determination in human behavior.* Springer.

coachee about the reasons for learning and then the motivation. There should also be a clear understanding from both sides of what motivation really means. Most learners do not distinguish the 'flat reasons' from the passion, drive and fuel for learning: the 'motivision'. What vision does the learner have of their life when they can speak fluently? What would perfect English change in their life? For example, would it bring a promotion at work? A new job, maybe? Enhanced communication with a foreign boyfriend?

We should be aware that the reason for improving the target language may be the same as the motivation to improve; however, it could also be totally different.

Let me give you an example: I have a client who wants to travel the world. In this case, the reason and motivation for improving the target language could be to speak enough English to be able to travel the world. Even if I suspect it is the same, I would still ask a vision question: 'Just imagine, you can travel the world freely because you have the confidence and the ability to speak English fluently. How is that going to change your travelling?'

If I have a client who tells me their reason is to be able to speak more English at work, I need to connect my learner to a vision that goes beyond that reason. The client, when pushed to vision, may envisage a promotion or even leaving and relocating to another country. The skilled language coach will be able to ascertain if there is a greater intrinsic motivation lying beyond the surface reasons for learning.

If we think about the sports coach, they in fact have quite an easy job relating to motivation, because their athlete wants to break the record or to win the cup, run the fastest or jump the highest/longest. The Neurolanguage coach seeks to find the intrinsic motivision that is going to inspire the learner *so much* that they will want to attend the sessions and, ideally, will even do consolidation out of the sessions to be able to progress even faster.

This motivation conversation should be taken in a step-by-step manner, commencing with a diagnostic to find out exactly how motivated the coachee really is with a scale question (on a scale from 1 to 10, where is your motivation?). Then the coach would ascertain the reasons for the language, and finally there would be the push to vision question.

There are, in fact, three types of coachee:

1. The 'yes, motivated' or at least fairly motivated.
2. The 'not motivated, but there is something in my life which would motivate me to learn the target language'.
3. The 'not motivated, and nothing in my life which would motivate me to learn the target language'.

The 'yes, motivated'

If the coachee clearly has a reason to learn or improve the target language, the Neurolanguage coach should reformulate the reasons and then capture the motivision with a key vision question. Once the vision is ascertained, then, just like the sports coach keeps reminding the athlete of the winning of the cup or the breaking of the record, the Neurolanguage coach should keep referring back to that vision throughout the language learning process. This serves to inspire the learner and to consistently reconnect them with their chief motivation. It also acts as a pick-me-up: whenever the coachee is feeling down or unhappy with progress, the coach can use the vision to animate and encourage.

For example, I have discovered that my coachee wants to improve so that he will be considered for a promotion. I will check with my client if I can keep reminding him of this, using it as a 'motivision reminder' whenever I can to inspire, animate and keep that vision of the client getting that promotion alive! Honestly, in my experience, it acts as an instant inspirational tonic.

The 'not motivated, but there is something ...'

Many people do not really understand what their deeper intrinsic motivation is to learn the language, except for the fact that they want to learn or they need it for some reason, whether work or personal. They have probably never even really thought about what they could do if they spoke the target language fluently and what benefits this could bring to their life.

In addition, some people are forced to learn by their company. I personally had the experience of one company in Germany changing the company lingua franca to English and then forcing their employees to use it, consequently creating the need to learn it. Obviously, the employees felt this was unfair, and clearly motivation was lacking. In these particular cases, the Neurolanguage coach should compassionately acknowledge and recognise the unfairness of the situation, but at the same time should explain to the coachee that without motivation the brain might not learn effectively.

If the learner cannot connect with a 'work vision', the coach must steer the motivation conversation into other areas of the learner's life which could benefit from improved fluency. What could the learner achieve in their life with that language under their belt?

One of my coachees was one such learner and had been forced to improve his English. We circled on motivation and really found nothing that motivated him to learn. Then we moved into his hobbies, and he told me that he was a sailor and sometimes went on sailing holidays. At that moment, his whole energy shifted as it suddenly clicked that better English would help him when he was sailing in international waters. When I asked how he would feel if we looked at some sailing language and even how some expressions like 'learning the ropes' are used in business, he started to smile and became more interested, motivated and extremely curious. We had tapped into his motivision.

Another of my clients told me he would love to help his son with his English. When I said that was a super idea and we could really focus on getting him able to explain grammar and language areas to his son, he also notably shifted his energy and became very motivated.

Once the motivision has been found, as mentioned above, the

Neurolanguage coach will ask permission to use it and keep reminding the learner of it. For example, my sailor and I would sometimes look at the maps of his next sailing trips!

The 'not motivated and there is nothing ...'

Finally, we come to the scenario of the unmotivated learner who has probably been forced to learn, does not want to be there, has not found any benefit when we asked and therefore has not connected to any motivision whatsoever.

At this point, I would get out the honesty card! I would explain that motivation really is an essential ingredient of the learning process and, without it, the learning process will probably not be effective. As no intrinsic motivation has been found, I would then steer the conversation to the learning process. How do you want to learn? In other words, what activities could inspire you? What would stimulate you enough to actually want to come to our sessions every time?

I had one particular learner who was the perfect example of a 'no motivation to learn English' client. We touched base on his motivation at the beginning when we started to work together and then periodically thereafter. He was a top medical officer for a multinational and fully recognised his need for English at work. On the other hand, he blatantly admitted he hated English and was not at all motivated to learn it, and confessed that he never would be.

Whenever we had this conversation, he would always say that I, as his coach, was the motivating factor! He confessed he enjoyed our meetings, as they centred upon fascinating medical conversations, his work requirements and topics of interest and focus. The process that I was engaging him in was his chief motivation.

He was my client for ten years! He had a brilliant C1 level, and we probably met once or twice per month. And I have to say I always felt quite proud to have kept him connected to the language all these years, even as a 'not motivated' client!

Mechanical goal-setting

After ascertaining the motivision of the learner, the coach explains to the learner that Neurolanguage Coaching works on two different types of goals: the mechanical goal-setting, which deals with everything to do with the grammar, structure and pronunciation of the language, and the mastery goal-setting, dealing with the functional language or the application and use of the language. The reason we separate the process into two different goal types is to activate different learning states in our learners.

By focusing and working on grammar, we want to use critical, analytical thought and discussion to help the learner to connect with and use the theory. These are the mechanical goals, and the client chooses activities to work on these grammar goals. If we refer to Timothy Gallwey and his distinction between the thinking and the performing brain, in the mechanical goal part we want our learner to be engaging with the 'thinking brain'.[140]

On the other hand, the mastery goals focus on situations and scenarios and the functional language used in these. The idea here is to get our learner to come into the expressions and language naturally and to learn how to 'let go and let flow'. The learner sets mastery goals and activities to practise these, and in this respect we are provoking the 'performing brain'.

At this point, we transition into the mechanical goal-setting. Just as a caveat: if the learner has a low level of the target language, most of the initial session will be conducted in the native language. If the learner is extremely nervous, I would also recommend using the native language (except for the diagnostics).

The coach initiates the mechanical goal-setting by going into a 'diagnostics' conversation with the learner in the target language, so that the coach can hear how the learner speaks, constructs the

---

[140] Gallwey, WT (1974). *The inner game of tennis: The classic guide to the mental side of peak performance*. Random House.

grammar, uses the vocabulary and structures sentences. This diagnostics conversation should be conducted in such a way that the learner remains absolutely calm and relaxed, with no feeling of being tested, but at the same time the coach is skilfully taking the learner through different grammatical areas in the shortest time possible. This coach must know how to flow from present tenses to past tenses to future, to conditional etc., as well as to provoke other grammatical areas and check on the pronunciation. A highly skilled coach will also recognise what the learner is avoiding!

After the diagnostics, the coach should go into a feedback conversation. However, instead of immediately delivering their own feedback, the coach should first ask the coachee how they felt about that conversation and about the different grammar areas, and if there were any areas that felt better or weaker. Then the coach should ask if there are any grammar areas that the coachee would specifically like to focus in on, so the coachee can choose or highlight problem areas.

After this, the coach can then give feedback on what they have heard during the diagnostics conversation, highlighting the grammatical difficulties heard or the areas that were avoided, and checking whether the avoidance was due to lack of knowledge or uncertainty. If the coach has noticed a lot of grammar mistakes, it is best not to fire off a long list of mistakes, which could affect a learner's morale and destroy confidence. The coach can make a list for their own reference and highlight the most critical areas or those that make sense to tackle first, as they could be fundamental areas that need correcting.

At this point, both the coach and the coachee have given feedback, and various grammar areas should have come to light. Now the coachee should be asked which areas they would like to set as the first mechanical goals to be worked on. It is best to get the coachee to select one or two mechanical goals, which will later be put together with a couple of mastery goals. This is to ensure that the learner is not overloaded with goals and that the areas are chunked down so that focus and attention can be optimised.

As mentioned above, the lower the level of the learner, the more the mechanical goal-setting will take place in the native language, with just a short diagnostics conversation to hear any target language knowledge. Obviously, if the learner is a complete beginner then the conversation regarding the mechanical goals will centre around how to bring in a step-by-step learning process to block-build the language from scratch.

With a beginner, the key is to start with the grammar that gets the learner speaking the fastest. For example, in English this would necessarily be the verbs 'to be' and 'to have', the impersonal 'there is' and 'there are', and the formulations of questions and negatives of these. Then it would be a case of step-by-step building the language, introducing present continuous as the real present and the present simple as the facts and habits tense. Clearly, in the case of a beginner, the expertise of the Neurolanguage coach will be to steer those initial mechanical goals. In fact, the lower the level of the learner, the more the coach has to input.

When a learner has a higher level, the coach must get the learner to identify, choose and set their mechanical goals so that the learner really 'owns' those goals. This aspect of ownership is a very important player for the brain. The more that somebody feels that they themselves have set their own goals, the more likely they will be to actually achieve them. Research emphasises that when students set their own goals, they are more likely to take responsibility for their learning, which fosters empowerment and proactive behaviour.[141]

The mechanical goal-setting process is absolutely essential to establish the grammatical goals that the client wishes to work on.

---

[141] Elliot, AJ, & Fryer, JW (2008). The goal construct. In Shah, J, and Gardner, W (eds) (2008). *Handbook of motivation science*. New York: Guildford Press, 235–250 and Turkay, S (2014), Setting goals: Who, why, how? Manuscript. Accessed June 7, 2017, from vpal.harvard.edu/publications/setting-goals-who-why-how

Mastery goal-setting

After the mechanical goal-setting, the conversation moves into the mastery goal-setting process. This involves an in-depth conversation with the learner to find out what exactly they want to use the language for, and to establish the functional language for that specific application. The coach should steer the conversation from very general reasons for learning and generic language to much more specific and focused functional language, which can then be transformed into specific goals. The coach has to skilfully break down what the learner is saying and cocreate a list of areas to serve as the desired functional language goals.

For example, let us imagine that our coachee is a lawyer and wants to improve their English when speaking with clients. The Neurolanguage coach would ask questions to uncover what the lawyer discusses with clients, how those conversations go (in order to identify the functional language), what the lawyer feels is their weakest part of the language, and then the most important conversations to improve on initially. For example, questions like:

> ➢ 'May I ask you what types of conversations you have with your clients?'

> ➢ 'What area of law do you practise in?'

> ➢ 'I'm hearing that you deal with contract law. What parts of that technical language do you feel you would like to improve?'

> ➢ 'When you say you work with contracts, what does that mean? OK, so I am hearing that you need to draft them and then negotiate with the other party or parties. Could these two areas be potential goal areas to work on?'

> ➢ 'In the negotiation, how could we break down the different parts of that conversation? So, you mention that, to start with, both parties set out their arguments, and then you move into persuasive language. Could we put these down as potential areas?'

> Then, just to clarify: 'I understand that you explain contract terms to your clients, you also negotiate contract terms, and you mentioned that you draft the contracts. So, which of these do you feel you would like to focus in on first?'

Once the coach has steered the conversation into a chunked-down potential goals list, they should ask the coachee to choose which goal or goals they would like to set and work on as the first mastery goals.

Next steps after the goal-setting

By now, the coachee has set both mechanical and mastery goals and the coach should introduce a conversation regarding the actions to achieve those goals. 'Actions' means the active practical steps or learning activities the learner will engage in in order to achieve the goals.

This question should be posed to the coachee, who can decide on what activities they would like to perform to achieve the goals. This triggers learner autonomy and ownership. It will also ensure that the learner chooses preferred activities, normally activities that they enjoy doing, and this will ensure the right brain chemistry for learning!

There may be learners who really have no idea what activities they would like to engage in and turn back to the coach to say, 'You are the teacher – you tell me.' In this case, the coach should explain to the learner that the idea is to find activities and tasks that the learner enjoys, because we know that the more positive and fun they are for the brain, the more engaged the learner is and the more positive chemicals like endorphins and dopamine will flow, assisting in memory retention. If the coachee really has no idea, the coach could ask permission to create a menu of suggested activities for the learner to choose from.

During the goal and action setting, the most important factor is to empower the coachee to feel that they are in the driving seat, setting those desired goals and actions and then working to achieve them.

Once goals and actions are set, the next question to ask is regarding the time period to work on the goals. Coaching necessarily has a realistic point of time in the future when a goal review will take place. If no time period is set, there is no coaching process; it just becomes the eternal wish to achieve process!

For example, there may be two mechanical and two mastery goals together with some activities, and the learner may decide on a period of three months to work on these. Maybe this learner decides to meet the coach once a week for an hour, so in total there would be 12 sessions to work on the goals before the coach and coachee sit and do the goal review to check if the goals have been reached or not. This could be considered a reasonable period of time. If the coachee were to do consolidation work at home on top of this, then the learning process would potentially become faster and more effective.

If the coachee were to suggest an unrealistic period of time, either too short or excessively long, then the coach should have a coaching conversation to ascertain a more realistic time frame.

Should the coachee suggest an extremely long time period in our example above – say, one year for four goals – then the coach could suggest having interim reviews at intervals of perhaps one month or two months just to check in on where the coachee feels they are with regard to each of the goals. This interim check-in normally gives an indication to the coachee of the progress they have made, and it could be that the coachee personally realises that the time period set was longer than necessary.

In any case, there should be mini check-ins every so often, or 'pulse checks', just to see where the coachee is with regard to the goals.

At the end of the given time period, the coach and the coachee will have the goal review conversation. In this conversation, the coach will deal with each goal individually and will check how the coachee feels about each one: whether the goal has been reached, and, if not, what still needs to be done to achieve it.

In the event that the goals have been reached, a new goal-setting will take place. There may even be a mix of newly set goals with perhaps one or two goals that the coachee feels have not yet been reached and still wants to work on. The goal review will lay out the new pathway forwards with the next set of chunked-down goals.

Just as an afternote, the main reason for setting both mechanical goals and mastery goals is to get the learner to apply the language as soon as possible. In the case of a beginner, getting that beginner speaking right from the beginning, even in simple sentences, will boost the motivation and the feeling of achievement and thus inspire the learner to want to learn more.

In most cases, there is a barrier to speaking a language. If we, as Neurolanguage coaches, can help break this barrier down right from the start, then we will be nurturing a confident speaker who is encouraged to come into the performing brain rather than the thinking brain.

Obviously, the coach is the language expert and, in some ways, the mechanical goals may be steered by the coach. The coachee will say what they would prefer to work on, but the coach will also, from time to time, be introducing totally new grammar areas to bring the coachee further and deeper into the language.

With an extremely advanced learner, there may be less focus on grammatical areas and more emphasis on the actual application of the language. In fact, extremely advanced learners are sometimes quite difficult to deal with, because they have often reached a place of complacency and just want to maintain the language. I often find that, in these cases, it is interesting to stimulate the advanced speaker to want to dive even deeper into greater fluency and native expressions and to really go deep into complex grammar areas, such as inversions or mixed conditionals in English.

So, we have seen how the 3Ms – Motivation, Mechanics and Mastery – really are the backbone of the first session with a Neurolanguage coach. After the first session, a tailor-made personalised roadmap can be created, and then the ongoing sessions will focus on working towards all of the set goals.

Giving structure and form to a Neurolanguage Coaching engagement

To achieve the art of Neurolanguage Coaching, there has to be a structured engagement. This structure is given through five core parts of the Neurolanguage Coaching process denominated the 5Cs.[142]

These five core parts are:

1. Concrete requirements.

2. Clear targets and commitment.

3. Coaching conversation throughout.

4. Connecting the brain and conquering barriers.

5. Completion of goals.

1. Concrete requirements

Above all, a Neurolanguage coach must meet the ethical guidelines and professional standards related to coaching and the International Coach Federation (ICF) coach competencies. As the Neurolanguage Coaching course is accredited by the ICF, we fully integrate the competencies into the structure and process.

ICF competence 1 sets out ethical guidelines and professional standards. This relates to the appropriate professional conduct with clients and of course includes confidentiality. Clearly, one of the first steps will be to make a contract with the client regarding the engagement, to be agreed and signed by both parties. It is also essential for the Neurolanguage coach to establish trust and psychological safety

---

[142] © Rachel Marie Paling 2012.

right from the start of the engagement (ICF competence 4). In this way, the coach creates a safe, supportive environment that produces ongoing mutual respect and trust throughout the engagement. This should be continuously demonstrated through personal integrity, honesty and sincerity, demonstrating respect at all times for the client's perception and unique learning style.

After the formalities have been established, the coach should check what the coachee actually knows about Neurolanguage Coaching, and offer an explanation if the coachee has no idea.

The next stage would be to explore the motivation. As we saw above, the motivision has to be ascertained right at the beginning of the process, as this will be the driving factor for the learning and the commitment.

A written level test may be sent to the learner prior to the initial session to provide insight into the learner's current level of the language. In the first session, this level test can be discussed, with feedback from both the coach and the coachee regarding the areas that were stronger or weaker.

The spoken diagnostics conversation, which the coach conducts in person with the coachee in this initial session, is absolutely essential. I also mentioned previously the importance of going through the feedback with the learner and how the learner should be active in the whole discussion.

2. Clear targets and commitment

Having completed the diagnostics, there should be a clear decision from the learner, who chooses and sets the mechanical (i.e. grammatical) goals. Throughout the feedback and goal-setting there will be continuous active listening (ICF competence 6), powerful questions (ICF competence 7) and coaching presence (ICF competence 5). The coach will also be constantly focused on facilitating client growth (ICF competence 8).

Regarding the mastery side of the language, the coach will then move into a coaching conversation following the funnelling-down principle, from generic to specific, to find out exactly what the learner would like to set as the concrete mastery goals or functional language goals. The goal-setting falls under ICF competence number 8, and in addition, after the goal-setting, there will be a skilled conversation to get the learner to design their actions or activities (ICF competence 8).

Both goal-setting processes will require a strong coaching presence as well (ICF competence 5). The coach 'remains focused, observant, empathetic and responsive to the client' (ICF competence 5.1) and demonstrates curiosity during the coaching process (5.2). The coach manages their own emotions to stay present with the client (5.3) and demonstrates confidence in working with strong client emotions during the coaching process (5.4). The coach is comfortable working in a space of not knowing (5.5) and creates or allows space for silence, pause or reflection (5.6).

There should be commitment from the coach and coachee, with a definite time period set by the learner alongside the desired frequency of sessions. The coach 'partners with the client to design goals, actions and accountability measures that integrate and expand new learning' (ICF competence 8.2).

At this point, the Neurolanguage coach has all the essential ingredients to craft and design the path forward. The coach creates a personalised roadmap, which skilfully factors in all of the learner's desired goals and actions over the chosen time period, carefully ensuring that material is repeated and revisited to facilitate long-term memory wiring (following spaced repetition).[143]

---

[143] Kapler, IV, Weston, T, & Wiseheart, M (2015). Spacing in a simulated undergraduate classroom: Long-term benefits for factual and higher-level learning. *Learning and Instruction*, *36*, 38–45. doi.org/10.1016/j.learninstruc. 2014.11.001

3. Coaching conversations throughout

Once the mechanical and mastery goals have been set, the time period and session frequency agreed and the personalised roadmap crafted, then the actual language coaching sessions begin. These ongoing sessions are active coaching conversations with great focus on the goals and actions, working to achieve the desired goals.

The predominance of quiet, brain-friendly coaching conversations, in a non-directive and non- demonstrative style, will ensure an extremely calm and tranquil limbic system. This in turn creates a potentially improved learning process, with more focused learning. It not only focuses on training the learner in the chosen grammar areas but also trains the learner to 'let go and let flow' and experience the 'performing brain' state.

The Neurolanguage coach will constantly be trying to mitigate emotional triggers which arouse a threat response and will endeavour to create a 'perfect' learning state. There will be a fluid interplay of active listening and powerful questioning, whereby the coach establishes a balance between the fine art of block-building and correcting mechanical (grammar) issues as well as reinforcing the mastery (application) of the target language.

So, coaching conversations are fundamental to the engagement and the language learning process.

4. Connecting the brain and conquering barriers

The principles of neuroscience, neuropsychology and emotional intelligence pervade the whole engagement. The Neurolanguage coach is consistently a provocateur and stimulator of neural connections. The coach becomes the omnipresent facilitator for the coachee to make connections and associations. In addition, there should be a constant awareness of emotional blocks or any other barriers that could trigger the activation of the sympathetic nervous system, which in turn could cause depleted resources in the areas crucial for critical thinking, learning and memorisation.

The language coach has to always be on their toes, creating a continuous flow of significant positive feedback: asking the right questions, keeping the client in tune with their emotions about learning, introducing new topics, practising the topics, consolidating and asking permission. It is a never-ending dance of language and coaching with constant interaction between coach and coachee. The coachee should always be stretched with exactly the right questions and situations to make them think about the language, about the grammar and how it compares to the native language, trigger words, expressions etc. The key to all of our sessions with our learners, in addition to sharing insights about the brain and learning, is the learner's involvement, their active participation, voicing their learner autonomy and taking ownership of their learning.

We also need to incorporate cultural use of the target language, as often culture and language go hand-in-hand. It really is an added bonus to language coaching when the coach has detailed knowledge and experience of the culture of the target language country. Throughout the coaching conversations, with this knowledge, the coach can often convey the reason for some things to be said in the manner that they are said – for example, the use of understatement in British English or the very direct manner of German.

Neurolanguage Coaching evokes awareness (ICF competence 7) and really allows the coachee to understand the rationale behind certain behaviour, expressions or structures, and in this way enables them to relate or connect better through an associative learning process.

Here is a summary of how to achieve constant brain connections:

> Chunk material down.

> Utilise reformulation as a mode of repetition from both coach and coachee.

> Check how your coachee prefers to learn.

> Pose questions that arouse positive emotions and motivation.

> Grab the full attention of the coachee.

- ➤ Aim for a goal-focused process to ensure attention and provoke motivation.

- ➤ Make it real, personal and relevant[144] for the learner.

- ➤ Change learning techniques constantly – the brain loves variety.

- ➤ Use humour and fun.

- ➤ Co-create material together.

- ➤ Carry out language coaching through storytelling[145] or anecdotes.

- ➤ Make learning easy to digest with order and structure.

- ➤ Include visualisation or visuals.

- ➤ Ask the coachee to evaluate the meaning of the new language and compare it to their own language.

- ➤ Ask the coachee to contextualise the information and then to apply it.

- ➤ Ask the coachee to use the language learnt by relating a personal experience, and ask them to then reformulate the information in a different way.

- ➤ Ask ongoing questions to trigger a recovery of learning content and facilitate more associations.

- ➤ Ask the right questions to get the coachee thinking more and connecting the language dots!

- ➤ Open up dialogues with the coachee about the brain and learning.

---

[144] Priniski, SJ, Hecht, CA, & Harackiewicz, JM (2018). Making learning personally meaningful: a new framework for relevance research. *Journal of Experimental Education, 86*(1), 11–29. doi.org/10.1080/00220973.2017.1380589

[145] Yuan, Y, Major-Girardin, J, & Brown, S (2018). Storytelling is intrinsically mentalistic: A functional magnetic resonance imaging study of narrative production across modalities. *Journal of Cognitive Neuroscience, 30*(9), 1298–1314. doi.org/10.1162/jocn_a_01279

➤ Troubleshoot learning difficulties or issues with coaching conversations.

➤ Help the learner to find solutions and strategies wherever possible.

➤ Check with the coachee when to give feedback about errors: immediately when they make a mistake, or after a sentence or a paragraph? Everyone is different!

➤ Ensure that the coachee is fully involved and engaged in the conversation.

➤ Acknowledge the coachee as frequently as possible to create positive feelings around the learning and give recognition that the coachee is making progress.

➤ Include spaced out testing/consolidation of vocabulary.

➤ Revisit learning material within a certain period of time to enable the retrieval of information and the enhancement of long-term memory.

➤ Establish trust and intimacy with the client.

➤ Instil coachee with confidence and provide them with a safe space to make mistakes.

➤ Always be aware of social pain issues or scenarios.

➤ Try to discover emotional issues and use coaching conversations to assist the coachee through them.

➤ Share your cultural experiences with the coachee if you lived in the target language country.

➤ Explain style and manner of speech so that the coachee can understand cultural implications – in particular formal and informal language structures inherent to the language, such as the 'polite you' forms in many languages.

5. Completion of goals

At the end of the designated time period, both Neurolanguage coach and coachee should come together for a review of the goals and ascertain whether the goals have been reached and how the coachee feels about them. Normally language checks and tests are performed, but coaching is about a subjective self-evaluation.

If the coachee feels they have indeed reached the goals, then the next step would be to initiate a new goal-setting process for both mechanical and mastery goals. If, however, the coachee feels that the goals, or some of the goals, have not yet been reached, the coach should explore whether the coachee would like to work further on these goals and, if so, for how long. The coach should also check if there may be some other activities that the coachee would prefer to engage in at this point, and/or whether the coachee would like to repeat actions that they chose previously.

As already explained above, the continual flow of setting goals, working towards these, then achieving them, reflects a spiral progressive learning process.

The learner may, after a period of time, decide to cease the engagement completely, and the coach could then conduct a final review of the goals and go through a feedback form to understand the effectiveness of the language coaching process.

*

We have now seen how the 5Cs lay down the structure for the Neurolanguage Coaching process. Accompanying this process, there should be adequate administration of the engagement. This should be reflected in forms that illustrate the mechanical goals, the mastery goals, the chosen actions, the time period and frequency, the individual sessions and the goal reviews. These forms will ensure that the entire process is extremely well documented and can serve as a record not only for the learner but also for the Neurolanguage coach to firmly keep track of where the learner is at any given time. The goal sheet forms may even be signed by both coach and coachee to really imprint the intention and the commitment of both parties to the entire process.

With the necessary documentation, and in particular with the goal review sheets, there will be a constant measurement of success and hopefully a constant feeling of achievement. Measuring success in language learning is extremely difficult in practice, as the normal way to measure success has always been the written test, which nowadays is mostly multiple-choice. Often, learners struggle the most with the spoken side of a language, which, obviously, is the most essential part!

The continuous focus on the spoken language in every single coaching session and in the goal review allows the learner to truthfully self-evaluate, and scale questions could be used to measure success. The more a learner feels that they are able to speak the language, the more motivated and inspired they will be to learn more.

We should also open up a conversation with our learners about the 'language plateau'. We have all experienced it, but no one really talks about it!

I always think the language learning process could be described as a step learning process, like a staircase, but not just a flight of normal steps! It really reflects those long tread steps which have a longer plateau than normal and then a short step up. This picture of a staircase in Sitges near the iconic church, Església de Sant Bartomeu i Santa Tecla, perfectly represents the long tread. I remember as a little girl I found these stairs really challenging!

Our learners may be stuck on a long plateau, experiencing a feeling of no progress for a long time. Then, out of the blue, we take a small step up; we start to feel that we understand more, we can speak more and we generally feel a difference. However, then it happens again: that feeling of nothing happening and no improvement, and we find ourselves on the next long plateau, feeling despondent and depressed because we feel no progress. Suddenly, we go up another small step, and so on, and so on. This is the 'long tread, short rise' stairway to fluency, and achieving those goals along the way is the real reflection of that small step upwards that we take each time we improve.

This really emphasises the importance of frequent goal reviews, so that our learners can recognise and celebrate their small successes!

Long tread staircase, Sitges, near Barcelona

Part V

Delivering grammar and non-grammar through brain-friendly coaching conversations

The most prominent skill of the Neurolanguage coach is the delivery of *any* linguistic topic, grammatical or non-grammatical, through extremely calm, brain-friendly coaching conversations. In this way, the coach avoids the activation of the sympathetic nervous system and the threat response of the learner and, in addition, facilitates immediate connections and associations, as well as the instant application of the grammar in spoken language.

Research shows that the meta-competencies of non-directive coaching increase the frequency of creative insights and induce higher levels of creative ideas.[146]

PACT PQC[147] is a coaching model I have created which lays down the pathway for the coach to conduct these calm conversations. All coaching models provide the coach with a direction and path through a coaching conversation, almost like a mini script in the background.

The essence of this model is to direct the learner's brain through focused conversations, stretching the learner beyond their current knowledge or consolidating what is already known, introducing new material wherever necessary and provoking new connections. The key is the relaxed manner which provides a safe space for the learner and avoids the feeling of vulnerability. Our learners should feel that they can ask us anything along the way and that we are fully accessible and obliging to facilitate the learning.

---

[146] Bartolomé Anguita, GB, Vila Almenara, S, Torrelles Nadal, C, & Blanco Calvo, E (2022). Right cortical activation during generation of creative insights: An electro-encephalographic study of coaching. *Frontiers in Education*, 753710. doi.org/10.3389/feduc.2022.753710

[147] © Rachel Marie Paling 2013.

The outcomes for the learner are greater confidence, improved language retention, and more creative use of language.

The model's name stands for:

P   – Placement

A   – Assessment

C   – Conversation

T   – Teach

PQ – Powerful Questions

C   – Clarification

The model should be used with flexibility; that is, not in a linear fashion. The coach will use each and every part of the model as they see fit, with a greater predominance of 'placement' and 'assessment', as these two are essential firstly to direct the conversation and secondly to ascertain the baseline of knowledge of the learner. In this way, the coach will adapt to the dynamic of that particular learner or learners (remembering that no two brains are the same!).

All aspects of the language should be chunked down by the coach first into a mini script which reflects the big picture of the area. According to the level and needs of the learner, the coach will then build it up, step-by-step, through the PACT PQC model conversation.

Now let us look at each of these parts of the model individually.

P – Placement

Placement means signposting. It is one of the terms that David Rock uses in his Dance of Insight coaching model.[148]

As language trainers, I think a lot of us have the experience of assisting learners with the delivery of presentations in a foreign language, and

---

[148] Rock, D (2007). *Quiet leadership: Six steps to transforming performance at work.* New York: Harper Business.

most of us have the experience of delivering presentations ourselves. If you can imagine the signposting language which is given when we deliver presentations, the idea is to constantly connect the audience to what is being presented. This is exactly the same type of signposting that we use with this model.

It is absolutely essential to indicate exactly what part of the grammar we are talking about at any given time. The coach must have a clear map of where they are taking that particular grammar conversation and must clearly signpost all the way through. This will ensure that both the coach and the coachee will constantly be at the same point in the conversation and the attention of the coachee will be maximised. One of the ladies who took my course called this 'GPS mapping', and what a superb way of describing it.

Research has proven that guided instruction is much more effective than discovery.[149] Our signposting is our way of guiding through the conversation, and this, coupled with summarising after each chunk, will ensure that our learners keep up with us.

Examples of placement could be:

> 'Well, in this session we are going to come in and focus on your first goal, which is "to feel more confidence when using the present tenses". How does that sound to you?'

> 'Firstly, let us begin with the present continuous ...'

> 'Now, how about we focus on the actual formation of the present continuous?'

> 'Super, now we have in fact covered the formation and you have done really well, and we're going to move on to how we formulate questions in the present continuous.'

> 'Well done, your questions are sounding really good, and now let's move the focus into the negative form of the present continuous.'

---

[149] Clark, RE, Kirschner, PA, & Sweller, J (2012). Putting students on the path to learning: The case for fully guided instruction. *American Educator, 36*(1), 6–11.

Signposting or 'placement' shows that there is a constant thread running through the conversation. Obviously, it is an invisible thread that the coach is very much in charge of guiding, and the main purpose is to keep both coach and coachee on the same track at the same time.

A – Assessment

The next step after signposting is to assess what the coachee already knows about this topic. This is because, as the coach, we need to find out exactly where the coachee is with their understanding and ability to express what they know. We need to know the baseline of their knowledge.

How the coachee responds will tell you exactly how much they know, will highlight potential misunderstandings or lack of knowledge, and may even indicate where mistakes are coming from. It will also allow you to hear doubts or confusion.

More often than not, as teachers we automatically launch into explanations of the grammar before exploring what our learner already knows. Our learner may already know it, in which case we have no need to even go into this part and we can move on to the next. In this way, we ascertain already acquired knowledge, and we avoid our learner feeling bored or frustrated because they are repeating areas they already know. If the learner does not know an aspect or is confused, then we move to the T: Teach.

Examples of assessment could be:

> ➤ 'Now, what do you know about the present tenses in English?'

> ➤ 'May I ask you how we form the present in English?'

> ➤ 'Could I just ask, firstly, how many present tenses are there? Super, can you tell me what they are?'

> ➤ 'Now, I hear you say that we have two presents in English, the continuous and the simple. Would you be able to tell me how we form these tenses?'

> ➤ 'How about the negative form of that tense – how is it formed?'

> ➤ 'And could you tell me about the question form?'

C – Conversation

After each assessment of a grammatical area, the coach engages the coachee in a practice conversation concerning the real life of the coachee to get them to practise the area being explored. Or the coach may ask the coachee for some example sentences.

This gets the coachee to connect with and implement the focused grammar, and apply the grammar instantly. In reality, the coach is checking that the coachee can in fact use it.

Mini conversations or asking for examples may be introduced at various intervals. There could be some conversation after the Assessment part of PACT to check if the coachee is implementing the language correctly, or after Teach, so the learner is instantly applying newly acquired knowledge and testing it out. So, these conversations serve the purpose of confirming what the learner already knows or immediately applying newly acquired information.

Examples of language to introduce conversations could be:

> ➤ 'Thank you for telling me about the present continuous. Now, let us put this into practice a little bit. Could you tell me what you are doing at the moment? What about your family, what are they doing?'

> ➤ 'And now let us move on to practise the present simple: may I ask you to tell me what you normally do on a Monday? What about at the weekends?'

> ➤ 'Now, we have just been looking at the formation of questions, so how about you ask me as many questions as you like?'

T – Teach

There will be times when the coachee demonstrates confusion or a lack of knowledge regarding a grammatical area. The session then becomes a dance between language teaching and language coaching, and at this point the Neurolanguage coach must use their expertise as a teacher and introduce new grammar.

However, whenever new material is introduced, the coaching style will ensure that it is not delivered in the traditional directive teaching style. This means a non-directive, calm, brain-friendly coaching style will prevail, ensuring that the learner remains calm at all times and thus open to receive and directly apply new knowledge. We introduce new information with a lot of permission and also in bite-size bits, so we avoid long explanations. I may even try to springboard from the coachee's native language by asking how they form that grammatical structure in their native language first and then gently introducing how it is in English. I would give some information and examples and then ask the learner to try out that grammar construct.

The Teach part of this model will only be necessary when there is a deficit in the knowledge of the learner or where a totally new grammatical topic is being explored.

Examples of Teach could be:

> 'Thank you for that excellent conversation on the present tenses. Now we have, in fact, discovered that there are some verbs that never take the continuous form in the present. How about if we introduce this particular grammar point and focus on this now?'

> 'So, we now know that there are in fact some verbs that never take the continuous form. Could we perhaps brainstorm some of these?'

> 'Well done, and yes, "to love" and "to hate" or "to dislike" are examples of these verbs. Now may I just give you some more, and how about if we get them into categories so that you can relate to them better? For example, we could create a category of

"emotional" verbs, as you already mentioned love, hate, dislike. Maybe we could also add "to like", "to need", "to deserve", "to prefer" – these are what we call "state" verbs as opposed to "action" verbs. Can you think of any more that we could add to the list?'

> 'You have superbly dealt with the state and action verbs. Thank you for that. I would like to go one step further now, if I may. There are, in fact, some verbs that can be both action and state verbs – were you aware of that? OK, so I'm hearing that is new for you. How about if we explore some examples together? First, let's take the verb "to weigh". Now, can you tell me when I would say "I am weighing something" and when I would say "it weighs"? What other verbs do you fit into this category?'

Interwoven with the PACT part of the model at all times is the PQC aspect: Powerful Questions and Clarification.

PQ – Powerful Questions

There are two types of powerful questions that will pepper these coaching conversations whenever the coach feels they could be useful.

The first type is powerful coaching questions. These could check in on the emotions or needs of the learner. For example, how are you feeling with this? What do you notice here? How can I help you with this? What bridge could you create to remember that?

The second type is questions that provoke native/target connections.[150] These stimulate the learner's curiosity to understand whether there are associations or disassociations at play. For example:

> 'How similar is this grammatical issue to the same issue in your language?'

---

[150] Weber, K, Christiansen, MK, Petersson, KM, Indefrey, P, & Hagoort, P (2016). fMRI syntactic and lexical repetition effects reveal the initial stages of learning a new language. *Journal of Neuroscience, 36*(26), 6872–6880.

> ➤ 'How could you build a connecting bridge to this word to help you remember it?'

> ➤ 'Let us connect the tenses to your language. How similar are these tenses to the tenses in your language?'

> ➤ 'How is that said in your own language?'

> ➤ 'What differences are there between this and your own language?'

> ➤ 'What similarities are there between this and your own language?'

> ➤ 'I notice that you said X; could it be that this is similar to your own language?'

> ➤ 'Let us try and understand where this mistake is coming from.'

> ➤ 'How can we disconnect this word so that you do not think of the German word when you see it?'

> ➤ 'How could you say that in a different way?'

> ➤ 'What is another word which means exactly the same as that word?'

> ➤ 'What is the opposite of that word?'

> ➤ 'Can you give me alternatives to that word – maybe three or four?'

C – Clarification

Clarification should be used to clarify what the coachee has said, if necessary. As coaches, we often reformulate what we hear in different words, so that the coachee may hear back what they have said in a different way. This allows the coachee to verify what they said. In addition, it brings in a new set of vocabulary and expressions, which enriches the learning process, allowing the learner to hear, learn and form associations with new variations of the language. In other words, clarification could be used to assist the embedding of the learning or genuinely to check for meaning and understanding.

Examples of clarification could be:

> 'Am I hearing that ...?'

> 'So, what you are saying is that ...'

> 'In other words, you mean ...'

> 'So, that is to say ...'

> 'Am I right in thinking that you mean ...?'

> 'Ah, that means ...'

> 'If I say this in another way, then ...'

> 'Let me put this in a different way. In fact, I am hearing that ...'

> 'That sounds like ...'

In essence, the PACT PQC coaching model will allow the Neurolanguage coach to perform a dance between coaching and teaching through any linguistic topic, grammatical or non-grammatical, in an extremely calm and relaxed and therefore enjoyable coaching conversation.

The skilled coach will come in and out of all of those parts of the model to really maximise the conversation and connect directly with the grammar in such a way that there is an instant application and comprehension.

Behind this model, the Neurolanguage coach is an absolute expert at chunking down any grammar topic. We now know that if we chunk grammar down into bite-size pieces, the brain will be able to deal better with this step-by-step build-up of language.

As language teachers we have never really created 'big pictures' of grammar areas, and I would suggest that this should be the first step prior to the coaching conversation. We create a big picture and break it down into a step-by-step buildup. This breakdown creates the pathway through that topic.

If we take an example of how to break down the present as a grammar area and carve out a step- by-step buildup, I can then use each part of this breakdown as my signpost when I go into the conversation with the learner. The higher the level of the learner, the more that will be covered in one or two conversations. If I have a lower level learner, I would potentially only do the first parts; that is, introducing the present continuous, formation, uses and trigger words and then the present simple, formation, uses and trigger words.

Present tenses breakdown

a) Introduce the present continuous tense:
- Formation: to be + -ING.
- Introduce the question form.
- Introduce the negative form.
- When is it used?
- Introduce the trigger words/indicators to show that the present continuous should be used.

b) Introduce the present simple:
- Formation.
- Care to be taken with the he/she/it endings.
- Spelling rules for the -S or -ES endings?
- Introduce the question form – verb DO/DOES.
- Introduce the negative form – verb DO/DOES.
- When is it used?
- Introduce the trigger words/indicators to show that the present simple should be used – brainstorm a list of these words.

c) Compare/contrast present continuous and present simple in easy contrasting sentences.

d) Introduce state and action verbs:
- Discuss the differences between these types of verbs.
- Brainstorm a list of state verbs and categorise wherever possible.
- Brainstorm a list of verbs which can be both, but with passive/active feel, e.g. 'to weigh'.
- Brainstorm a list of verbs which can be both, but which have different meanings according to the tense, e.g. 'to see': 'I see a dog' vs. 'I am seeing my friend this evening'.

e) Introduce the idea that both present simple and present continuous may also be used as future tenses.
- Present simple as future.
- Present continuous future.

Each grammar conversation will flow with its own dynamic and according to each individual learner. No two grammar conversations will ever be the same.

We have seen how the PACT PQC model can be used as the backbone for a coaching conversation around any linguistic topic. By moving grammar into brain-friendly coaching conversations, I have found (and so have the trainers who have certified with me) that the learner remains calmer, feels more empowered to understand and apply the grammar, and even starts to enjoy talking about grammar.

I would always recommend moving away from books when with a learner. Books can be used for self-consolidation and self-study, but grammar should be brought alive through interactive, relaxed, curiosity-evoking conversations!

In my second book, *Brain Friendly Grammar*,[151] I go into more detail about PACT PQC and in addition provide many different examples of ready-made breakdowns. In my third book, *Language Coaching in Action*,[152] I provide brain-friendly materials and the PACT PQC example conversations that can be used when we are co-creating the materials with our learners.

---

[151] Paling, R (2020). Brain friendly grammar: Neurolanguage Coaching. Express Publishing.

[152] Paling, R (2023). *Language coaching in action: Brain-friendly materials using Neurolanguage Coaching.* Choir Press.

Final word from the author: the way forward

Over the past twelve years, just over 1,700 language teachers have taken the Neurolanguage Coaching certification course to become certified and accredited Neurolanguage coaches. I am extremely grateful to everyone who trusted in this certification programme and really took on board its philosophy and message. Now, more and more language teachers are curious about how to change their style of delivery and the whole language learning process.

We live in an increasingly globalised world, and somehow we need to inspire not only children but also adults, whether from the private sphere or the corporate world, to learn more languages in order to come into better communication with each other worldwide and on all levels. It is not enough to think that English is the predominant language in the world; it should also be commonplace for English natives to learn other languages, and I sincerely admire people who *do* master another language, or languages. I, myself, have been lucky enough to acquire French, Spanish, Italian and German as well as some Catalan, basic Russian and basic Arabic. I would love over the next years to really master Russian, Arabic and Mandarin Chinese, even coming into Greek and Japanese. I would like to think that by the time I am 80 years old I will be able to speak ten languages or more.

My whole philosophy behind Neurolanguage Coaching touches upon the question of how we, as educators, can take the principles of neuroscience and coaching to enhance the learning process, helping our learners to learn better, faster and more efficiently with a brain-friendly coaching style. Through Neurolanguage Coaching we also build up our awareness of the impact, both negative and positive, we can have on a learner, and how as coaches we can fully empower our learners to succeed. I strongly believe in the potential of all of us to learn and develop as individuals and that throughout our lives we should never stop learning, as we now understand more about lifelong learning and neuroplasticity. The important factor is to enhance *the way* we learn. As we increasingly connect our understanding of the brain with how we as human beings learn, live and cohabit with each other, there is the hope that we will be able to shift forward into a new educational era: an educational era where learners are encouraged and supported at any age of their lives; where individuals are empowered and encouraged to be individualistic and to understand that everybody is different; where humans are able to apply lessons learnt to support each other and to really live the vision of a harmonious, plentiful, peaceful life for all.

Above all, in the new technological era, communication and language are key to our social interactions as humans. How we communicate can make all the difference. How we demonstrate and step up on our humanness will be key!

Finally, I wish you all great success in your Neurolanguage Coaching and learning, and I hope I inspire you to never ever stop coaching or learning languages.

If you talk to a man in a language he understands, that goes to his head. If you talk to him in his language, that goes to his heart.

Nelson Mandela

To have another language is to possess a second soul.

Charlemagne

For more information on the ELC Language Coaching certification course and all the Neurolangauge Coaching pathway courses, see aelca.academy and neurolanguagecoaching.com

Note about the author

Rachel M. Paling

Rachel Marie Paling is the CEO of Efficient Language Coaching and creator of Neurolanguage Coaching® and Neuroheart Education®. Rachel started teaching English as a Foreign Language to adults over 35 years ago. After obtaining a BA Honours in Law and Spanish (with distinction in spoken Spanish) in the UK, she did a Master's in Human Rights and Democratization (EMA) at the University of Padua, Italy, and Ruhr-Universität Bochum, Germany. She continued with her studies and qualified as a UK lawyer in 2003, but instead of pursuing a career as a lawyer, she combined her teaching experience, her specialisation in business English and her legal knowledge to language coach top executives across Europe. Through the years 2003 to 2011 she developed herself as a professional life coach and language coach. These crucial years helped crystallise her new approach, although she has continued to develop her life and language coaching up to the present day.

In 2012 she created a new approach (some have called it a method) for language learning called Neurolanguage Coaching® and began training teachers with one of the first ICF CCE accredited programmes for language teachers worldwide. To date she has trained over 1,700 language teachers worldwide and also delivers Advanced, Professional and Ongoing Sessions courses which carry the ICF accreditation. She has also trained 30 teacher trainers in her method and approach, who now are licensed to deliver in 12 different languages across the globe.

In 2020, together with ELC and Gary Houlton, she founded the Neuroheart Education Foundation and developed a new course for teachers of *any* discipline to become Neuroheart Educational coaches, to transform the educational process in schools, universities and corporates worldwide. This course is also accredited with CCE by the ICF.

She is a professionally trained coach with the ICF PCC Coaching Credential and is also a registered ICF Coach Mentor and certified Coach Supervisor. She holds an MA in Applied Neuroscience and a Master's in Neuroeducation and Neuropsychology, and is currently in a doctorate programme at Weatherhead School of Management at Case Western Reserve Univerrsity, Cleveland, Ohio, USA.

Also by Rachel Paling

Paling, R (2020). *Brain Friendly Grammar: Neurolanguage Coaching.* Express Publishing

Paling, R (2023). *Language Coaching in Action: Brain-friendly Materials Using Neurolanguage Coaching.* Choir Press

Paling, R (2015). *Chester the Vizla: I Believe in Miracles* (children's book). CreateSpace